# Grimsby Ontario Book 2 in Colour Photos, Saving Our History One Photo at a Time

Photography
by Barbara Raué
2017

Series Name:
Cruising Ontario

Book 186: Grimsby Book 2

Cover photo: 114 Gibson Avenue, Page 29

# Series Name: Cruising Ontario Saving Our History One Photo at a Time in colour photos

Books Available in Alphabetical Order:
Aberfoyle, Acton, Alton, Amherstburg, Ancaster, Arthur, Aylmer, Ayr, Bloomingdale, Brantford, Burlington, Caledon, Caledonia, Cambridge, Clifford, Conestogo, Delhi, Dorchester to Aylmer, Drayton, Drumbo, Dundas, Eden Mills, Elmira, Elora, Essex, Fergus, Guelph, Hagersville, Hamilton, Hanover, Harriston, Hespeler, Jarvis, Kingston, Kingsville, Kitchener, Linwood, Listowel, London, Lucknow, Mono, Mount Forest, Neustadt, New Hamburg, Niagara-on-the-Lake, Oakville, Orangeville, Orillia, Owen Sound, Palmerston, Peterborough, Petrolia, Port Elgin, Preston, Rockwood, Sarnia, Seaforth, Sheffield, Shelburne, Simcoe, Southampton, St. Jacobs, St. Marys, St. Thomas, Stoney Creek, Stratford, Thamesford, Tillsonburg, Waterdown, Waterford, Waterloo, Welland, Wellesley, Windsor, Wingham, Woodstock

Book 157: Brockville
Book 158: Merrickville
Book 159: Smiths Falls
Book 160: Portland, Newboro
Book 161: Westport & Area
Book 162: Perth
Book 163-166: Belleville
Book 167-168: Port Colborne
Book 169: Erin in Colour
Book 170: Goderich in Colour
Book 171: Sault Ste. Marie
Book 172: Lake Superior
Book 173-176: Thunder Bay
Book 177-179: Paris

Book 180: St. George
Book 182-183: Burford
Book 184: Mt Pleasant, Onondaga, Newport
Book 185-186: Grimsby

# Other Books by Barbara Raue

Coins of Gold

Arrows, Indians and Love

The Life and Times of Barbara
Volume 1: Inventions That Have Enhanced My Life
Volume 2: Entertainment That I Have Enjoyed
Volume 3: East Coast Trips
Volume 4: Olympics Have Always Intrigued Me
Volume 5: Wonders of the World
Volume 6: Caribbean Cruises We Have Enjoyed
Volume 7: Animals
Volume 8: Storms and Other Major Disasters in My Lifetime
Volume 9: Wars, Terrorist Attacks and Major Disasters

The Cromwell Family Book

Laura Secord Discovered

Daddy Where Are You?

Montana Series
Book 1: Montana Dream
Book 2: Life on the Montana Frontier
Book 3: Montana to Boston and Back
Book 4: Montana Sons Go to War
Book 5: Montana Sons Return From War

Visit Barbara's website to view all of her books
http://barbararaue.ca

## Table of Contents

| | |
|---|---|
| Ridge Road West | Page 6 |
| Mountain Road | Page 6 |
| Robinson Street South | Page 7 |
| Mountain Street | Page 8 |
| Elm Street | Pages 11, 30 |
| Murray Street | Page 17 |
| Nelles Boulevard | Page 17 |
| Livingstone Avenue | Page 23 |
| Gibson Avenue | Page 25 |
| St. Andrews Avenue | Page 31 |
| Adelaide Street | Page 35 |
| Elizabeth Street | Page 36 |
| Nelles Road North | Page 41 |
| Lake Street and Bell Park area | Page 43 |
| Architectural Terms | Page 56 |
| Building Styles | Page 60 |

Before written history, the Neutral Indians lived here. It was a perfect home with forests teeming with game, the lake providing fresh fish and transportation, and the fertile plain ideal for agriculture. The Neutrals were wiped out by their enemies by 1650.

In 1787, a group of United Empire Loyalists arrived from New Jersey. They named their little settlement The Forty after the creek which was believed to be forty miles from the mouth of the Niagara River.

John Graves Simcoe, an officer of the British army who served in the American War of Independence, became the first lieutenant-governor of Upper Canada (Ontario) from 1792-1796. The naming of the newly surveyed townships was part of his duty, and on a number of them he gave places names from Lincolnshire, England. One of these was Grimsby.

In the early days the many creeks on top of the Niagara Escarpment which flowed into Lake Ontario – each with a waterfall – were named according to their approximate distance from the Niagara River. There is the Twelve Mile creek, the Sixteen, the Twenty, the Forty, etc. It was along these creeks and stretching back from then on either side that the first settlers took up their land and built their log cabins, their saw mills and grist mills. This is how the Settlement at The Forty – later called Grimsby (from the name of the township) – began.

Less than twenty years after the arrival of the first settlers, the United States declared war on Britain and began by attacking Canada from three points – one of them was Niagara. In 1813, the Engagement at the Forty occurred on June 8, 1813. American forces, retreating after the Battle of Stoney creek, were bombarded by a British flotilla under Sir James Lucas Yeo. Indians and groups of the 4th and 5th Regiments Lincoln Militia joined in the attack and created such confusion in the enemy ranks that they abandoned this position and retreated to Fort George.

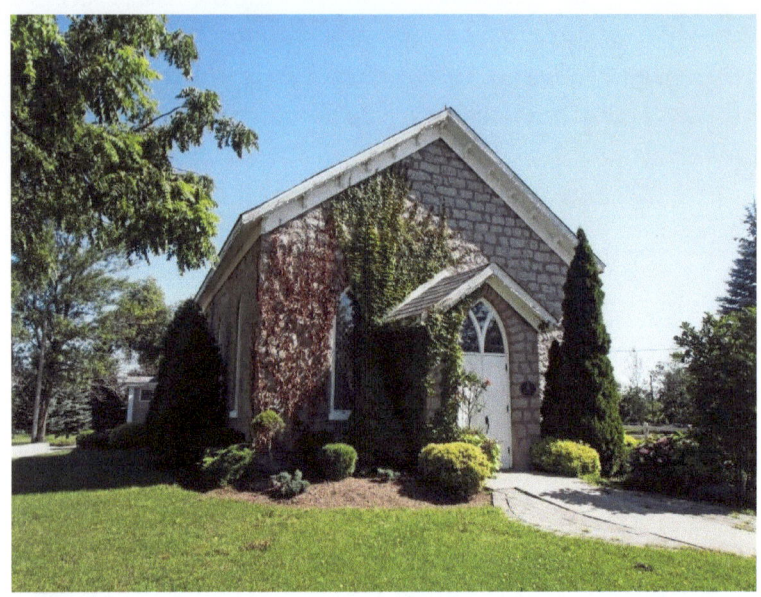

684 Ridge Road West – Rock Chapel United Church

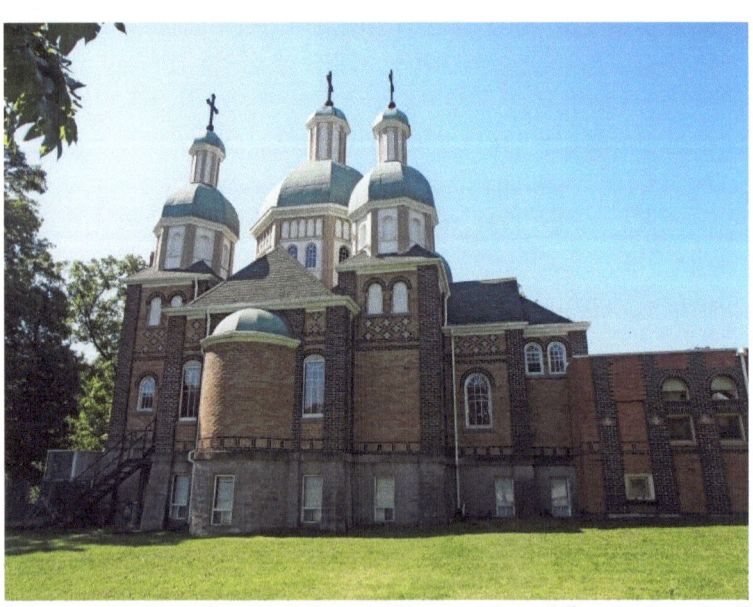

103 Mountain Road – St. Mary's Dormition Ukrainian Catholic Church – domes, cupolas, dichromatic brickwork

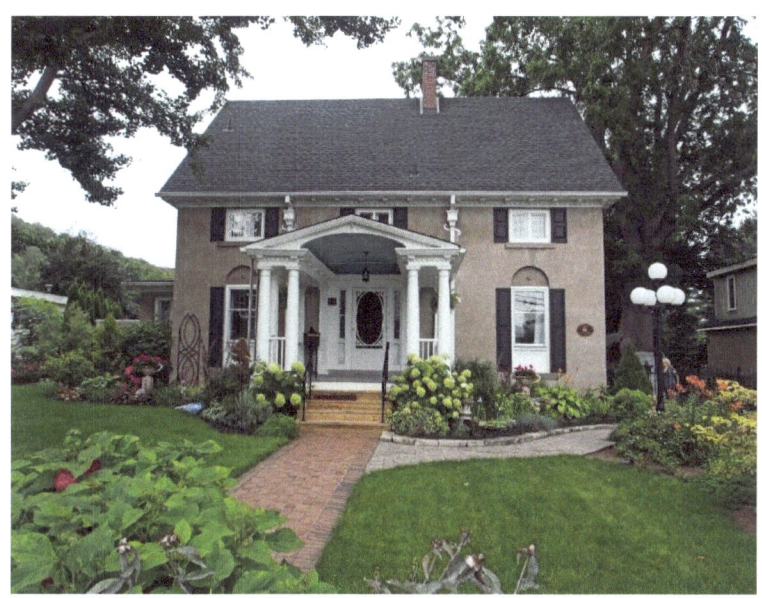

14 Robinson Street South – Helen Gibson House - Local quarryman and builder, W.F. Gibson, built the first two cement block homes in Grimsby at 14 and 16 Robinson Street South in 1912. In 1921, Mr. Gibson completely rebuilt 14 Robinson Street South. The building was reconstructed in the classical Georgian style with its long sharply pitched roof, internal chimney, symmetrical facade and centre hall layout. Plaster and stucco were then applied to the cement block. Dominating the front entrance is a Neo-Classical vaultro portico.

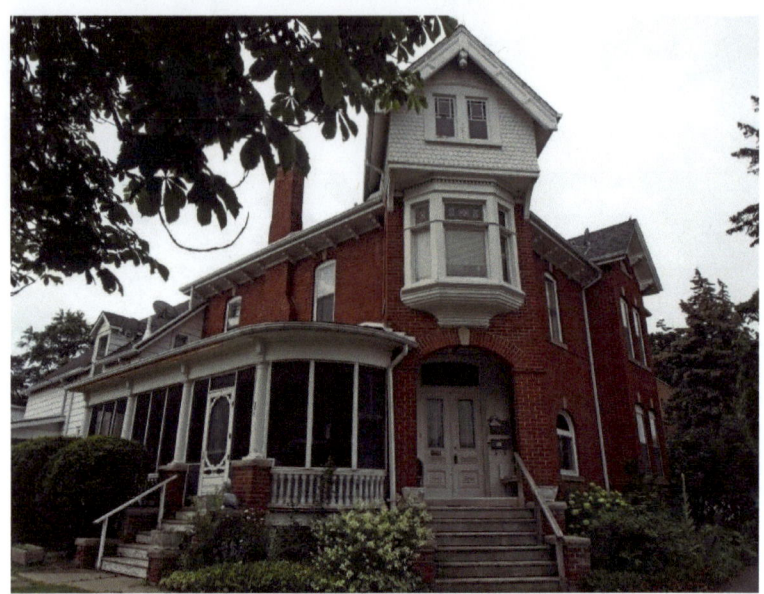
Robinson Street South – oriel window

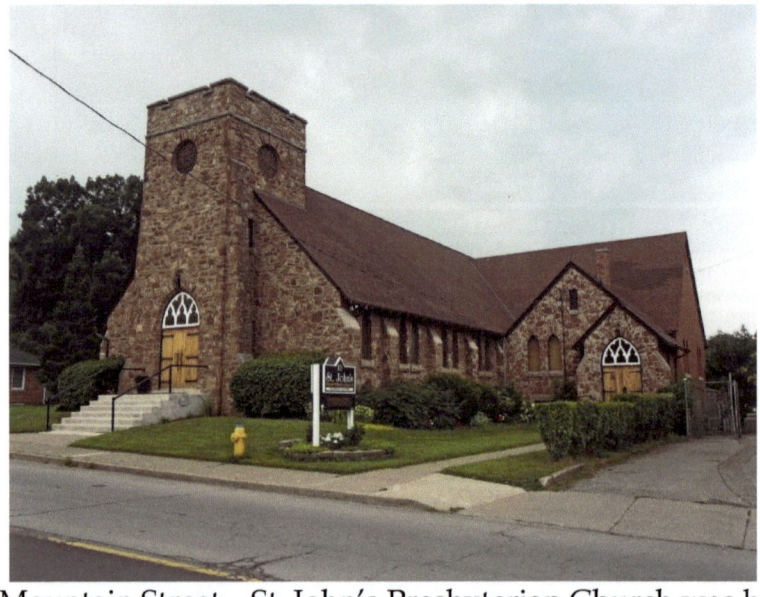
10 Mountain Street – St. John's Presbyterian Church was built in 1928 by the Shaffer Brothers, with the assistance of church members. Local red sandstone from Gibson quarry was donated by John Gibson, owner of the quarry.

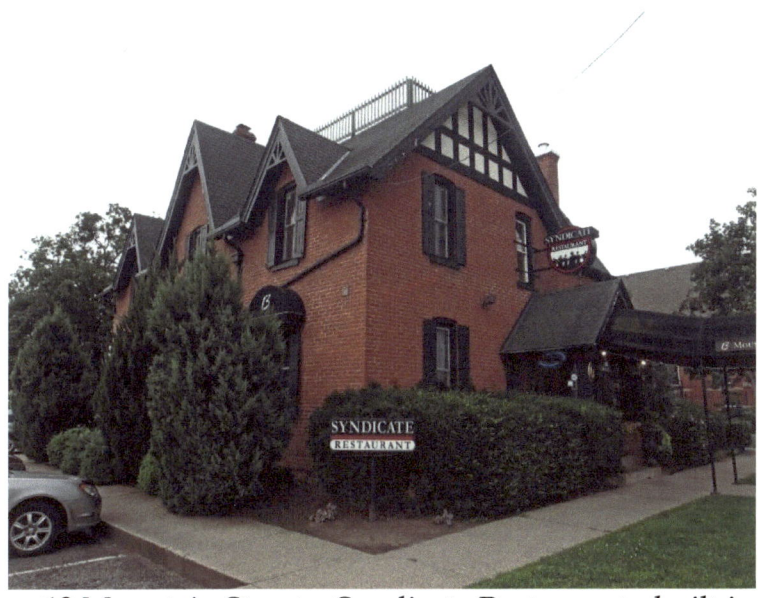

13 Mountain Street – Syndicate Restaurant - built in 1873 - This house was the home of Dr. Theoron Woolverton, one of the five sons of Dr. Jonathon Woolverton. Theoron was at university in the United States when the American Civil War broke out in 1860 and he joined the Army of the North as a surgeon. After the war, he continued to practice in the U.S. and raised his family there. His daughter Nina was born in the Brooklyn Naval Yards. Nina moved to Grimsby to live in her father's house, and upon her death, her brother Frank who also lived in New York, inherited the house. He married Lily Selby, a Grimsby woman who had taught in the Elm Street School for $350 a year. Lily had the sunroom added to the house and lived there until her death.

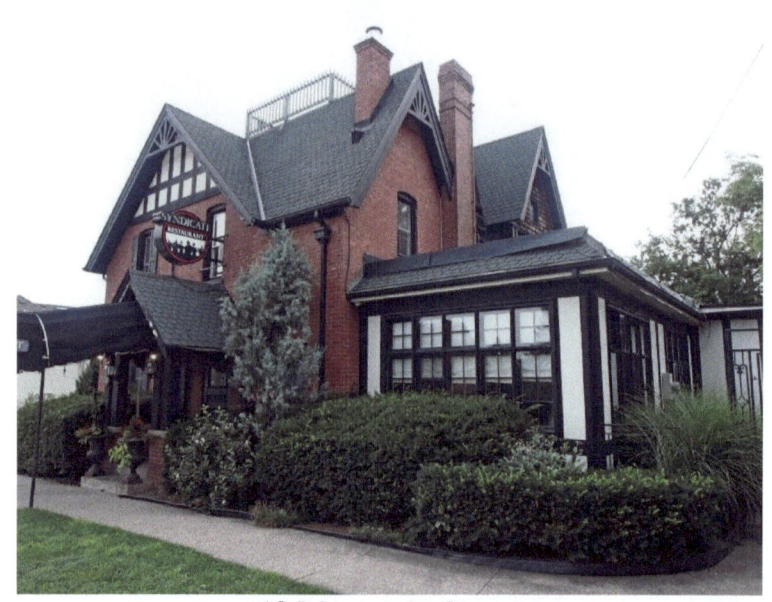

13 Mountain Street

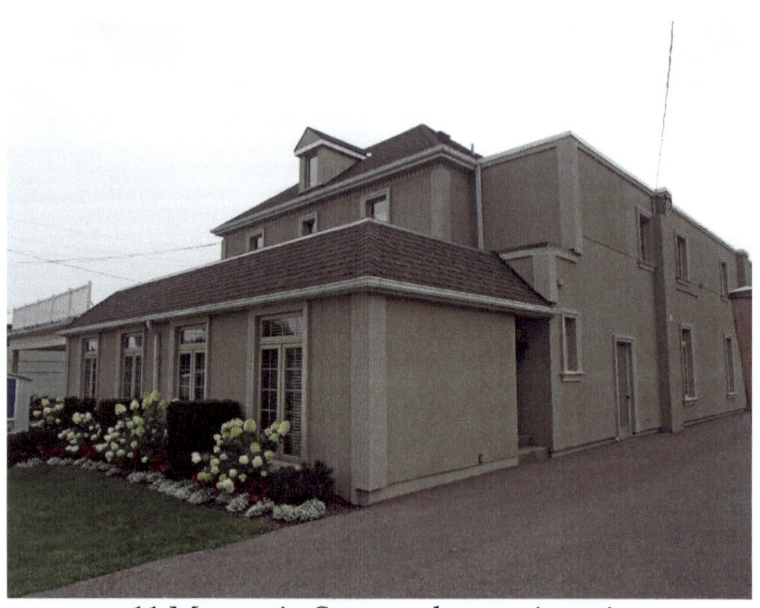

11 Mountain Street – dormer in attic

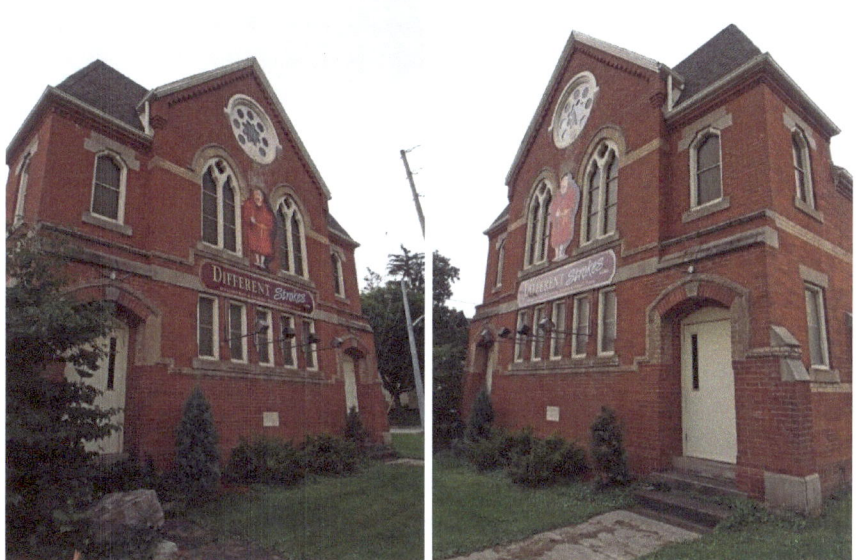

19 Elm Street – Different Strokes Pool and Billiard Hall – former Baptist Church built in 1880 - The original stained-glass windows including a rose window, the vaulted ceiling, and hardwood floors remain.

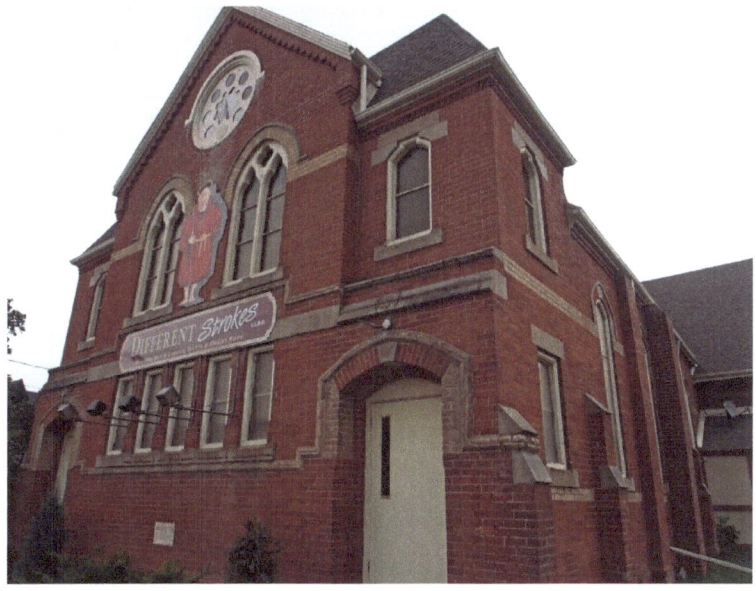

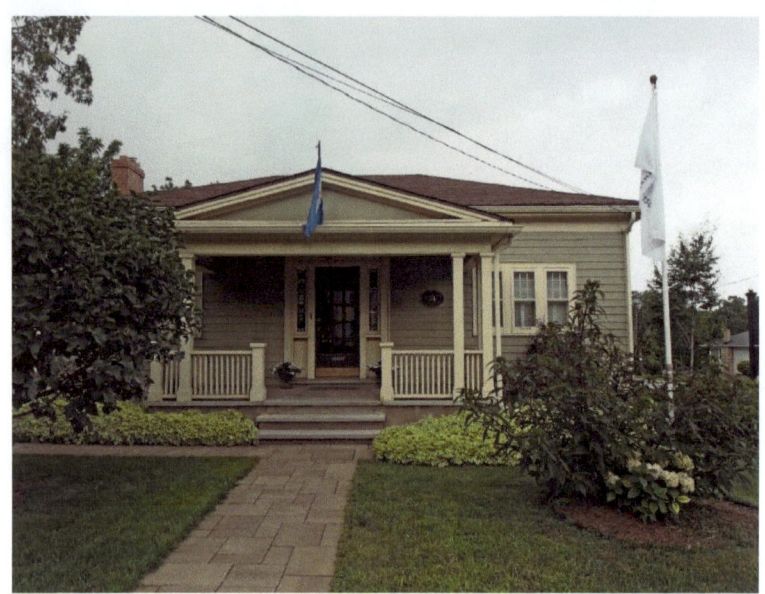

16 Mountain Street – Moore Cottage – This Regency Cottage was built in 1864 for Joseph Chambers, blacksmith and mason, who allowed part of it to be used as a private school. Later its owner was Bessie Kinzie Moore who owned and operated Moore's Theatre on Main Street East. It has a hipped roof and a pediment.

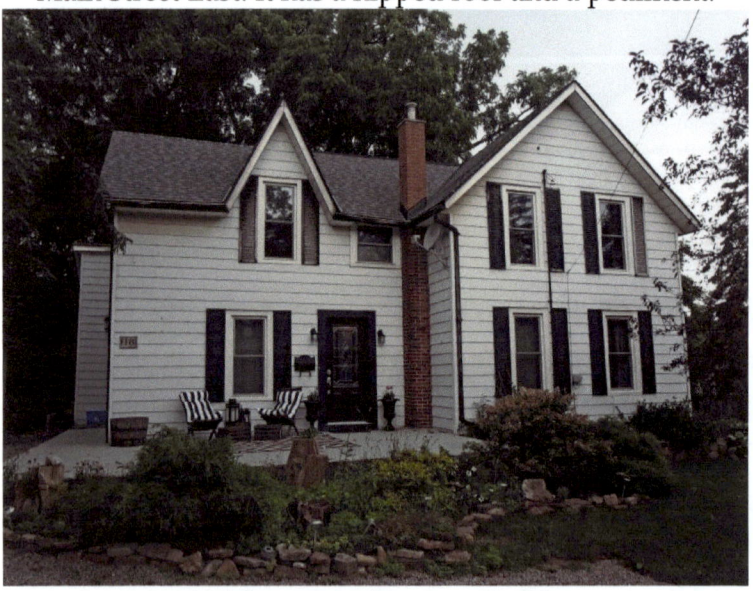

18 Mountain Street - Gothic

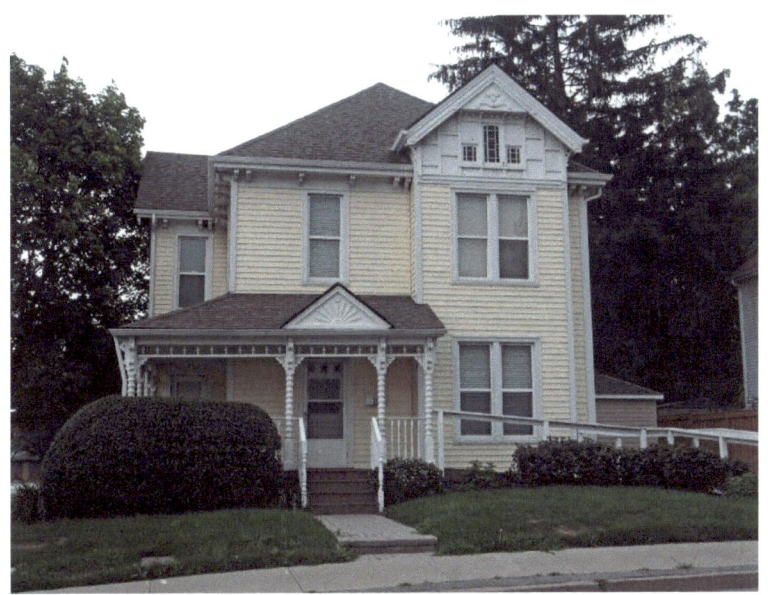

19 Mountain Street – 2½-storey frontispiece with Palladian window

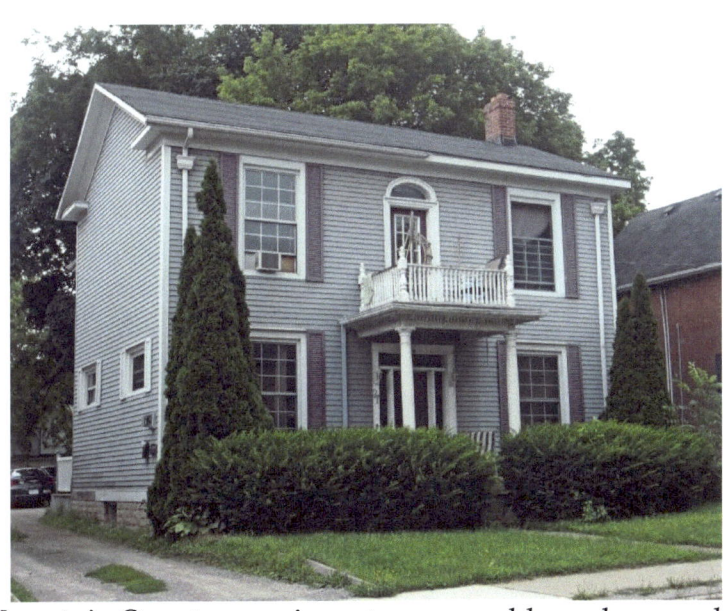

27 Mountain Street – cornice return on gable end, second floor balcony

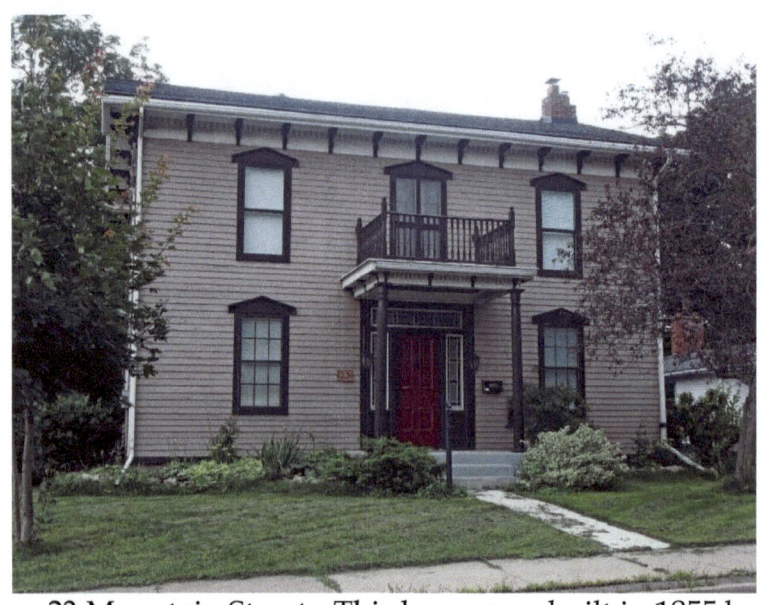

23 Mountain Street - This home was built in 1855 by John H. Grout, son of Reverend George Grout the rector of St. Andrew's Church. John became an important citizen, and entrepreneur who established the Grout Agricultural Works which manufactured reapers and mowers, the most modern farm machinery. He became a Reeve in 1876 when Grimsby became a town. Note the fine detail over the windows of the house and the stained glass windows framing the door.

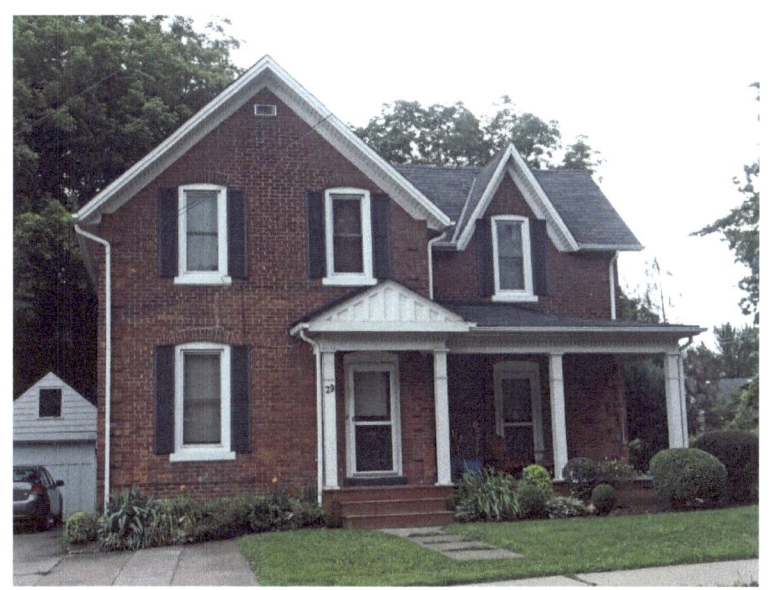

29 Mountain Street - Gothic

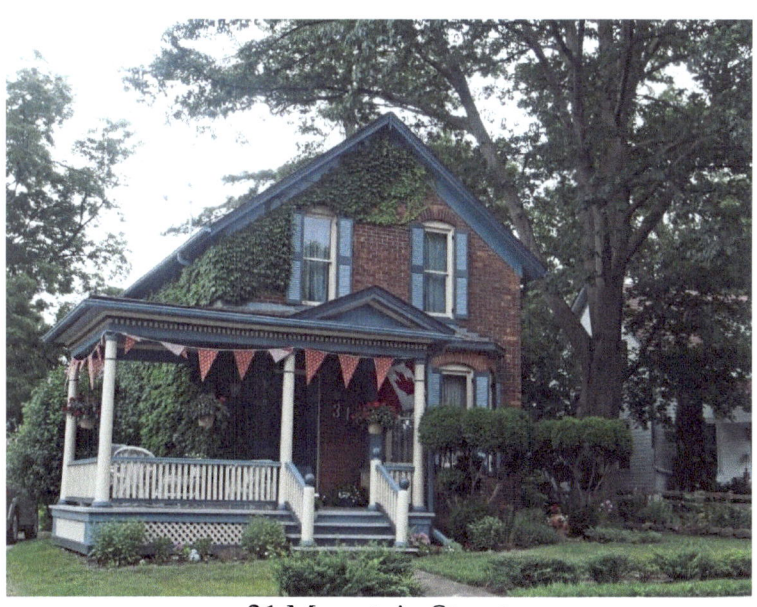

31 Mountain Street

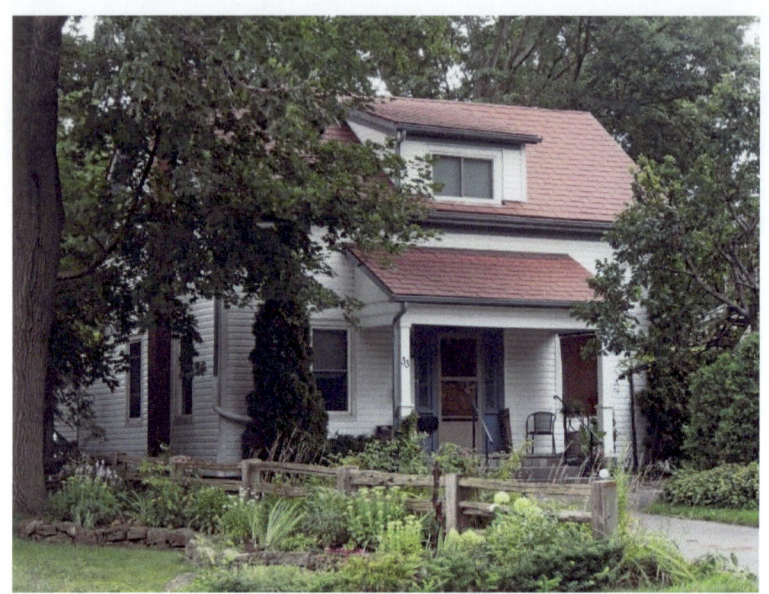

33 Mountain Street

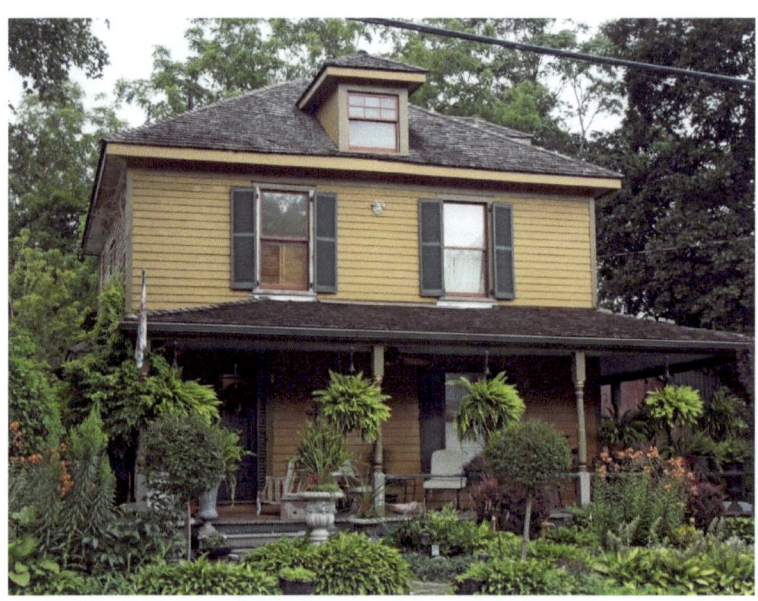

Mountain Street – dormer in attic

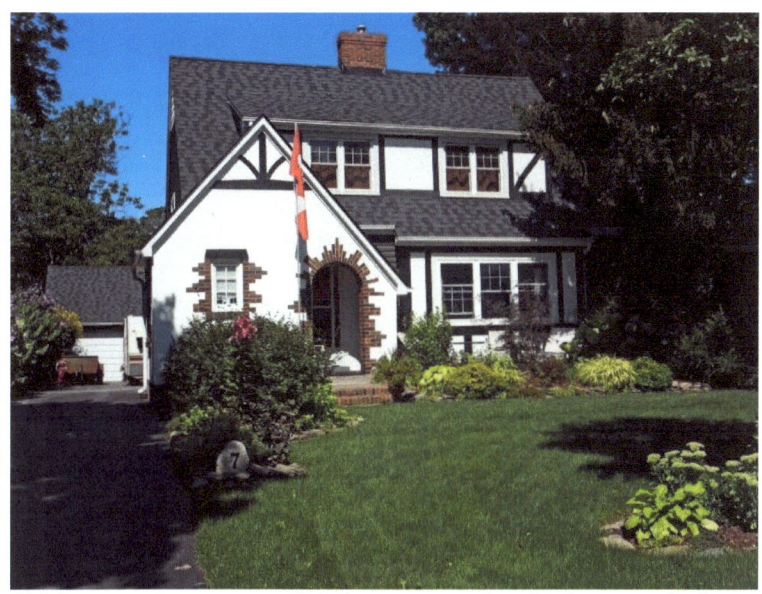

7 Murray Street – quoining around window and door

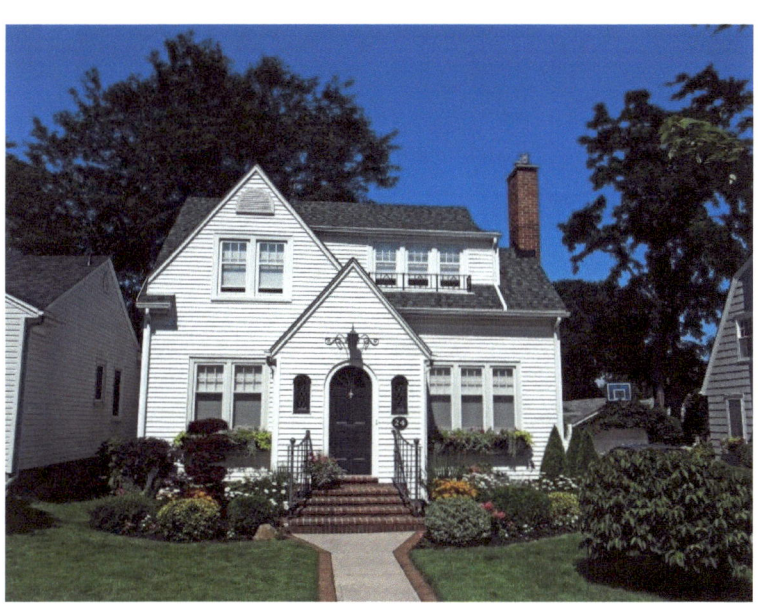

24 Nelles Boulevard

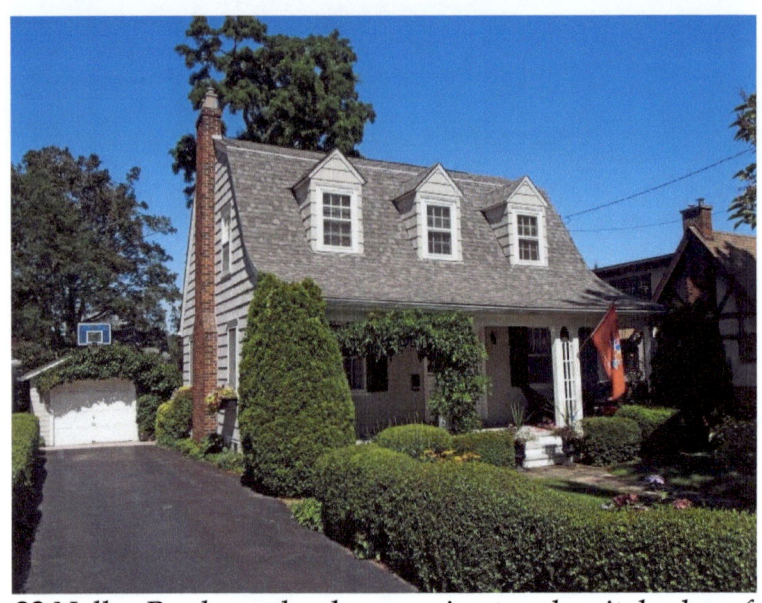
22 Nelles Boulevard – dormers in steeply pitched roof

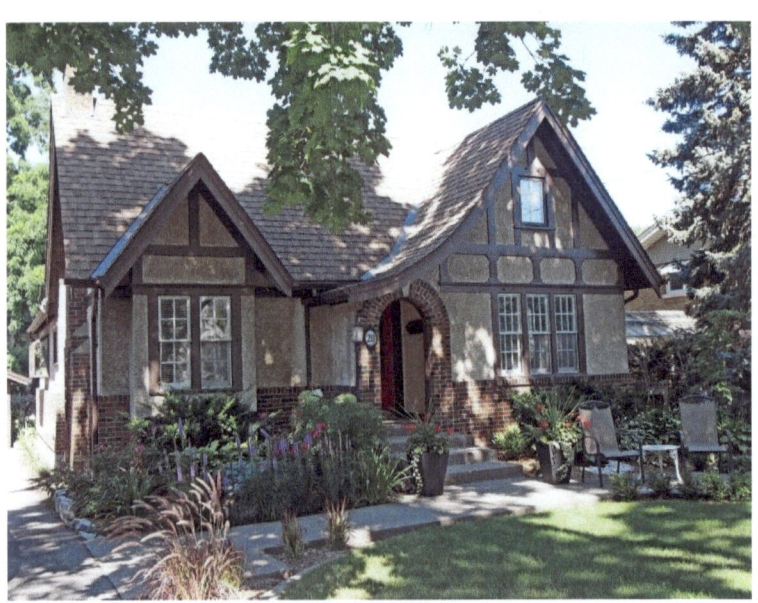
20 Nelles Boulevard - Tudor

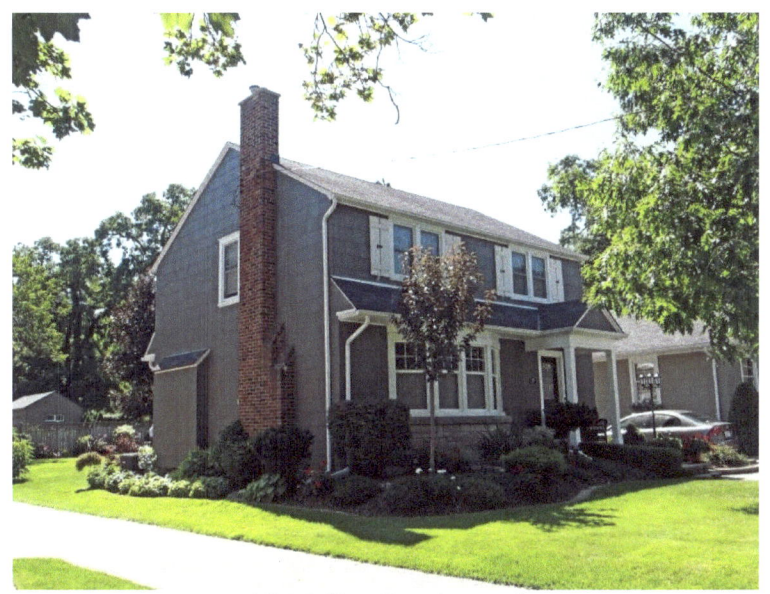

19 Nelles Boulevard

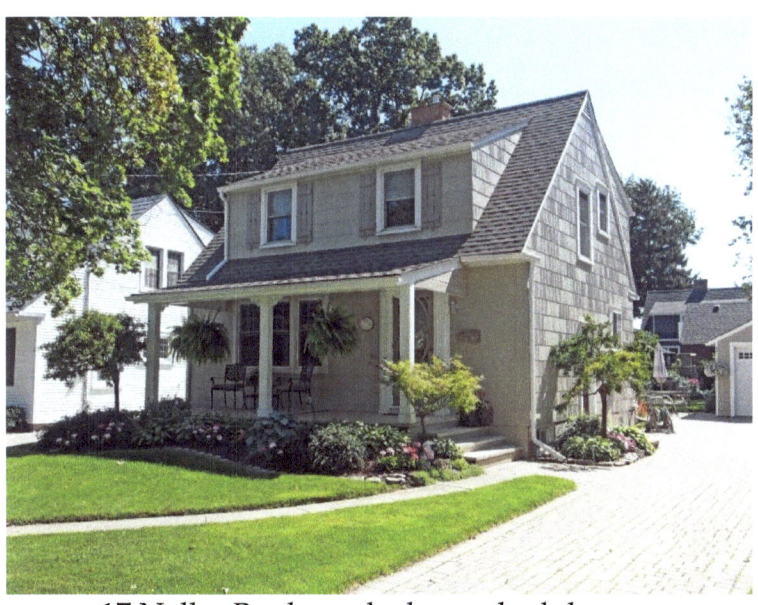

17 Nelles Boulevard – large shed dormer

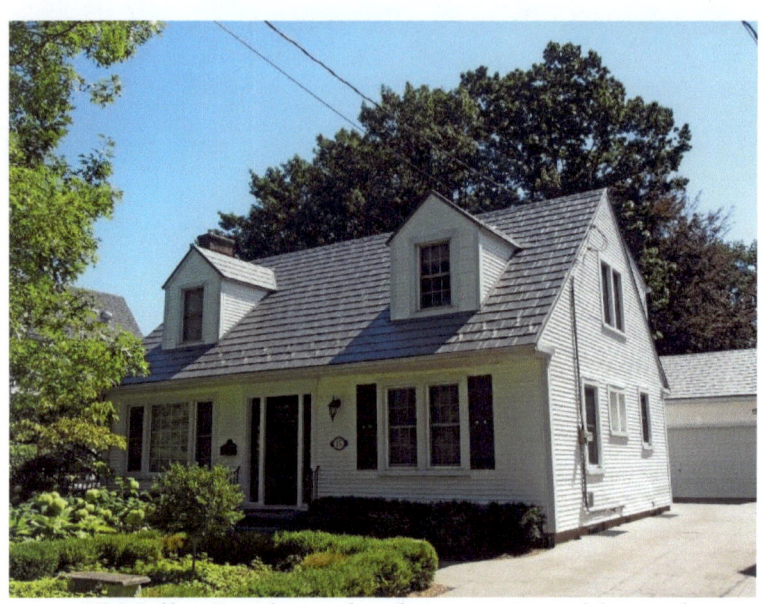

15 Nelles Boulevard – dormers in gable roof

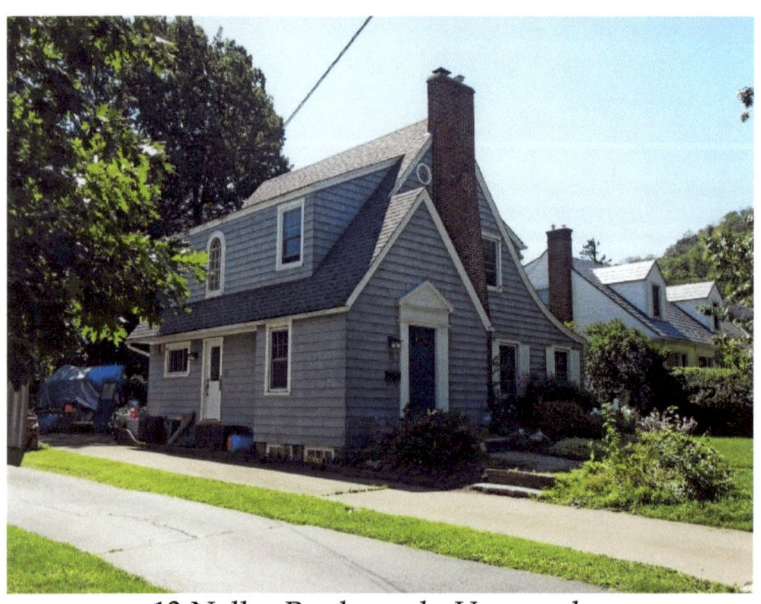

13 Nelles Boulevard - Vernacular

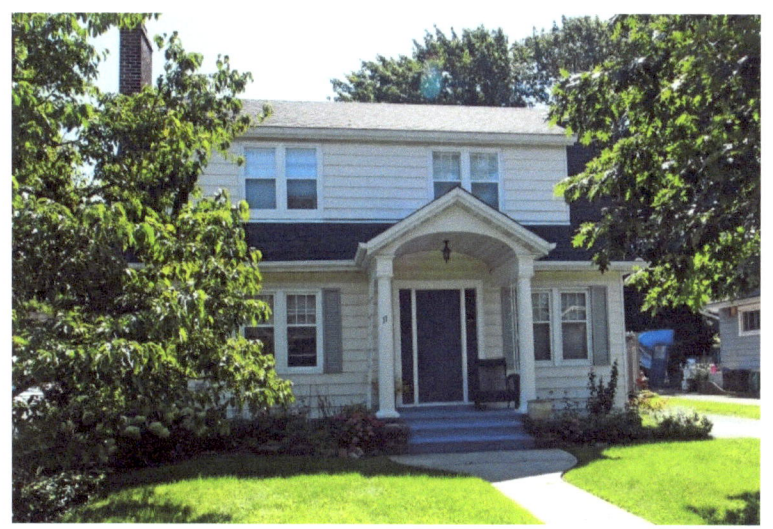

11 Nelles Boulevard – Neo-Colonial – gambrel roof, shed dormer

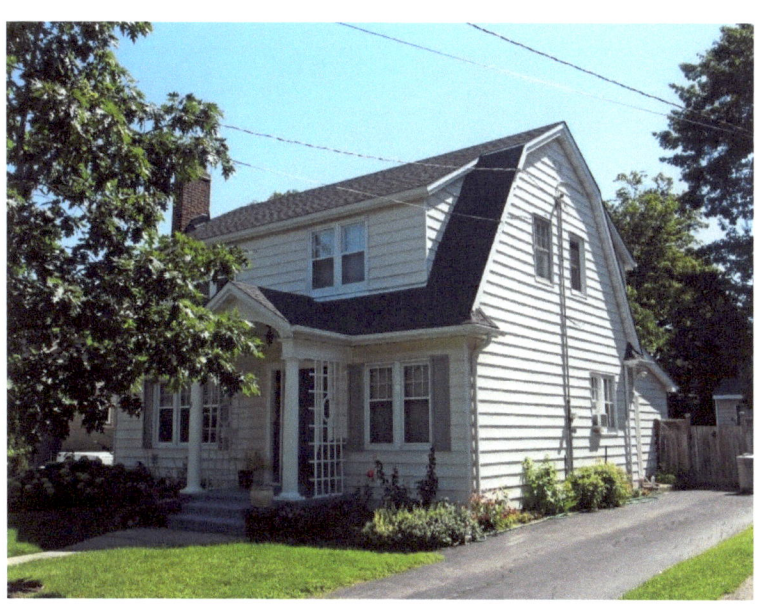

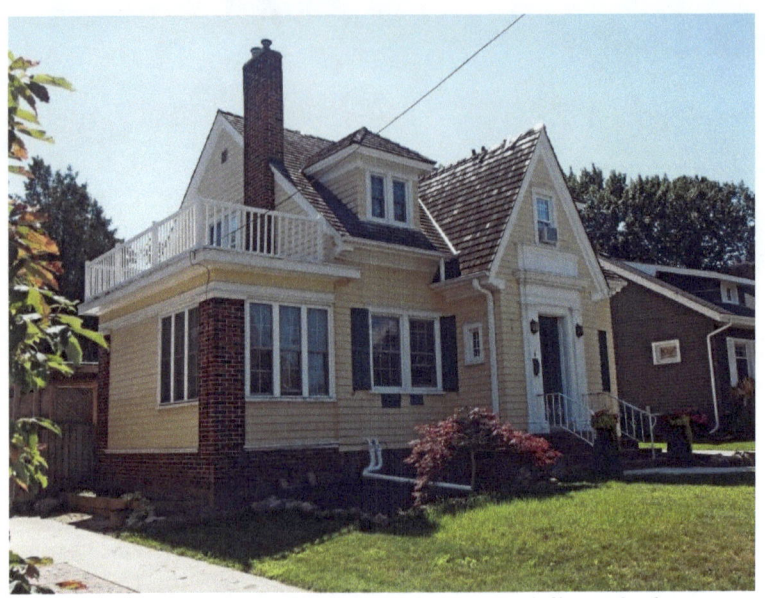

5 Nelles Boulevard - dormer, second floor balcony

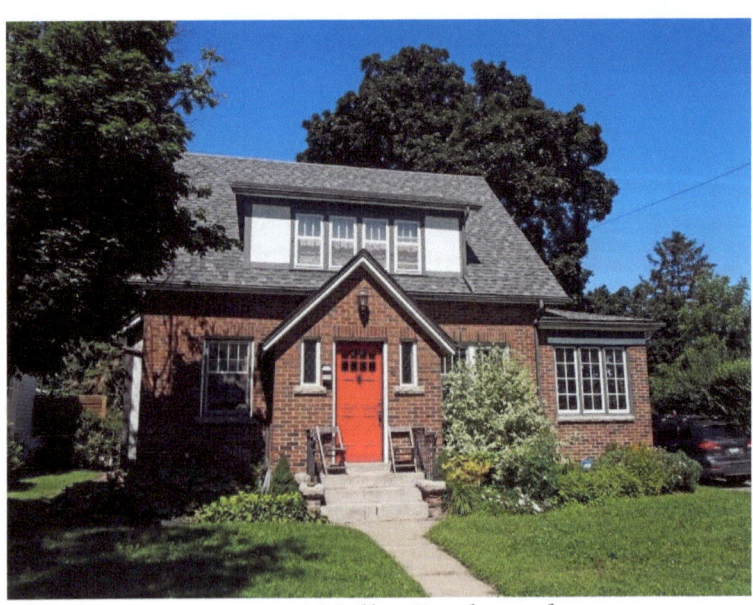

4 Nelles Boulevard

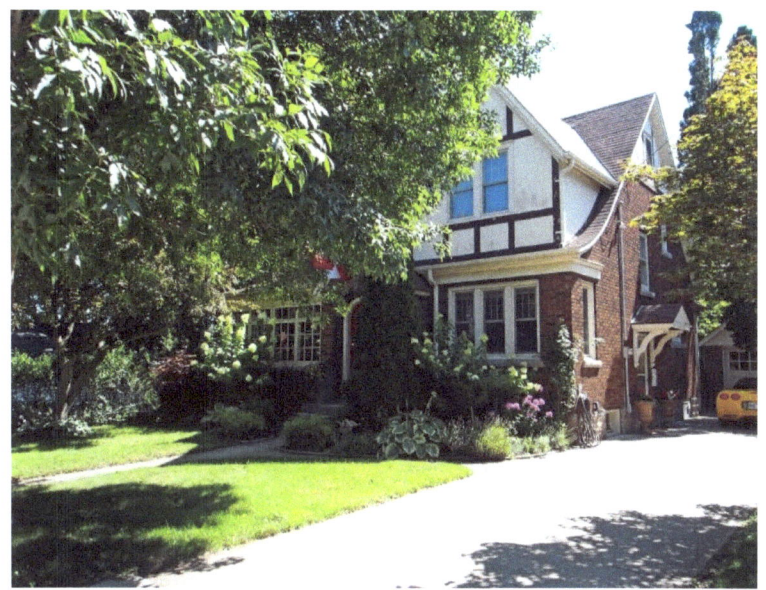

Nelles Boulevard - Tudor

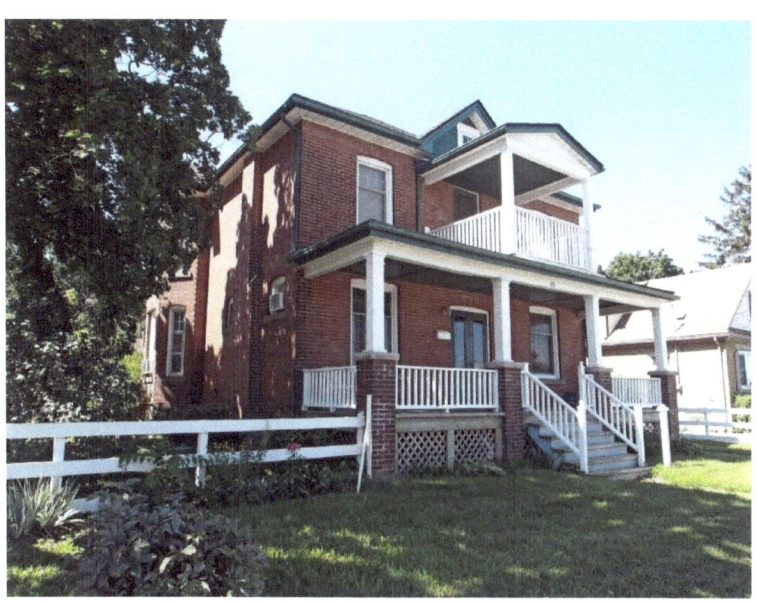

19 Livingstone Avenue

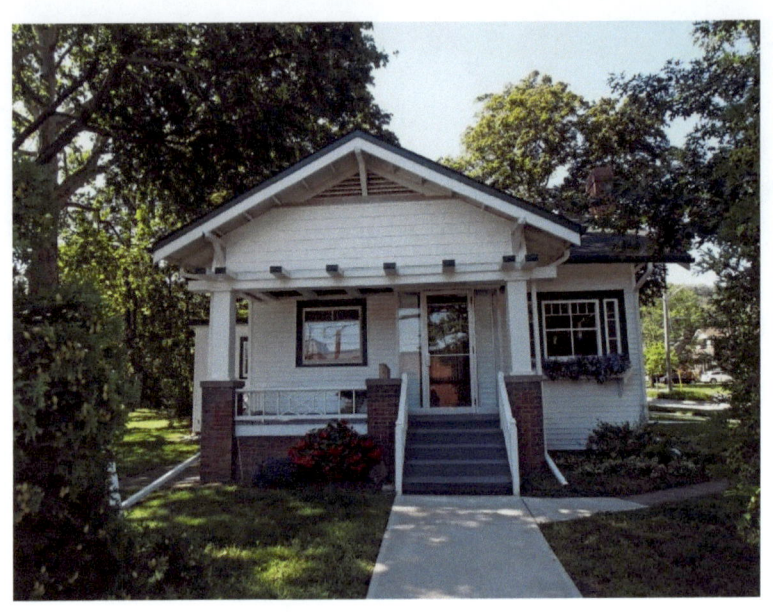

17 Livingstone Avenue

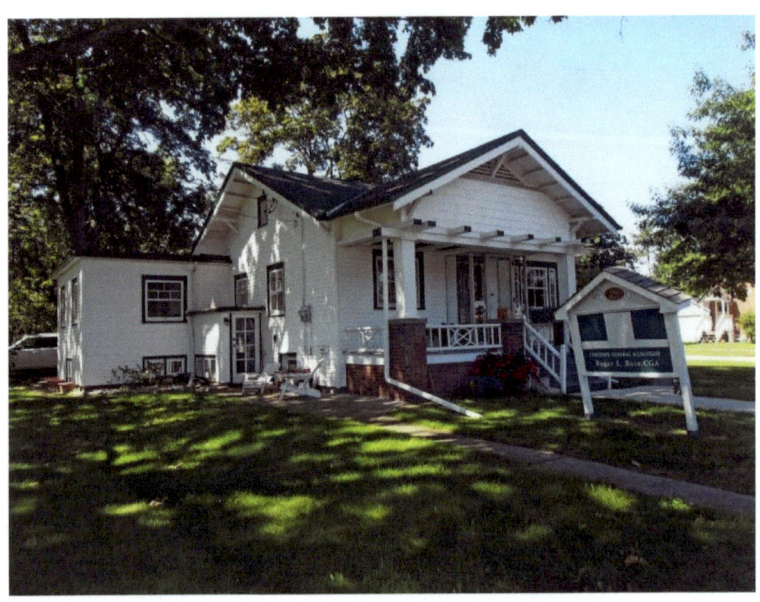

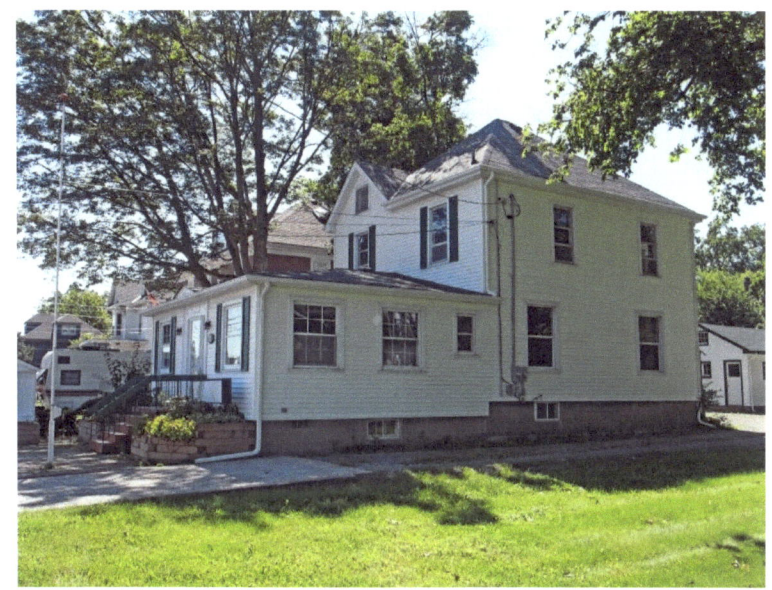

17 Livingstone Avenue

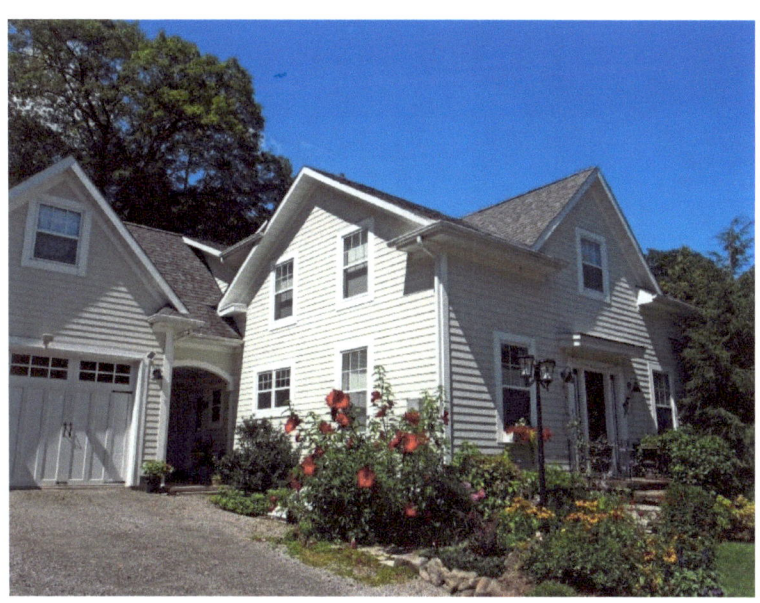

102 Gibson Avenue – cornice return on gables

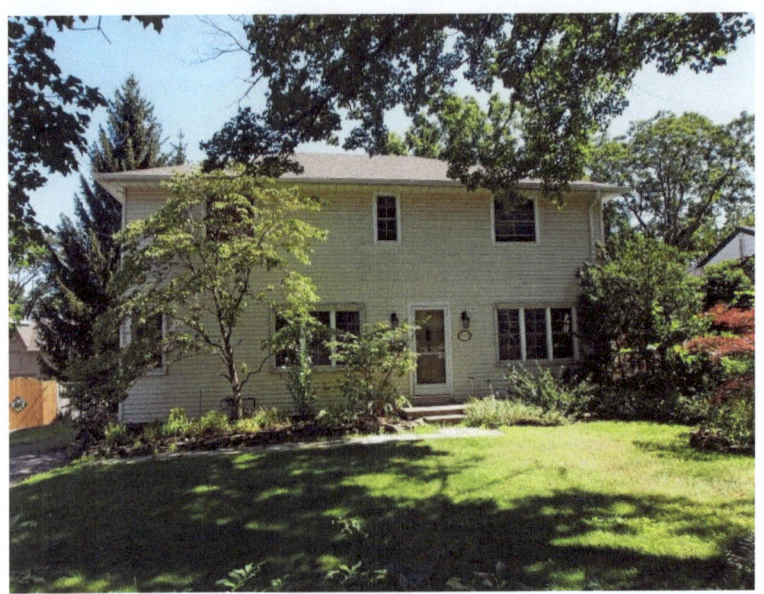

103 Gibson Avenue – hipped roof

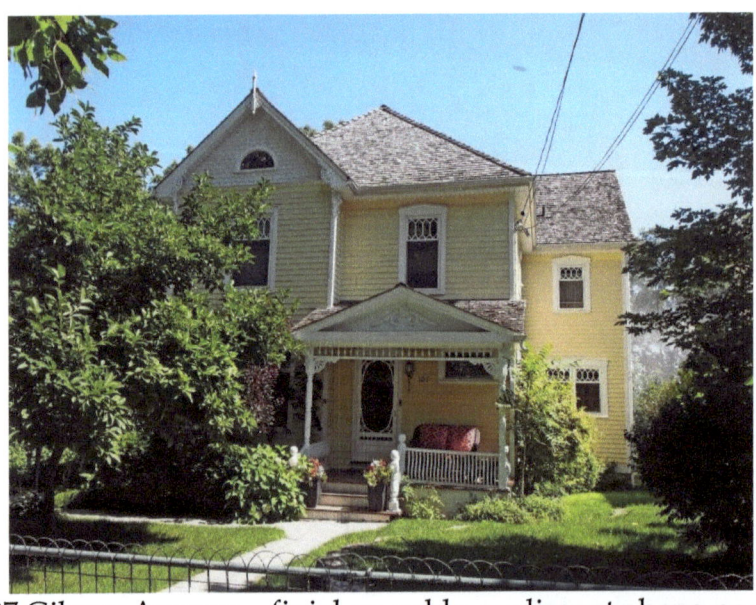

107 Gibson Avenue – finial on gable, pediment above porch

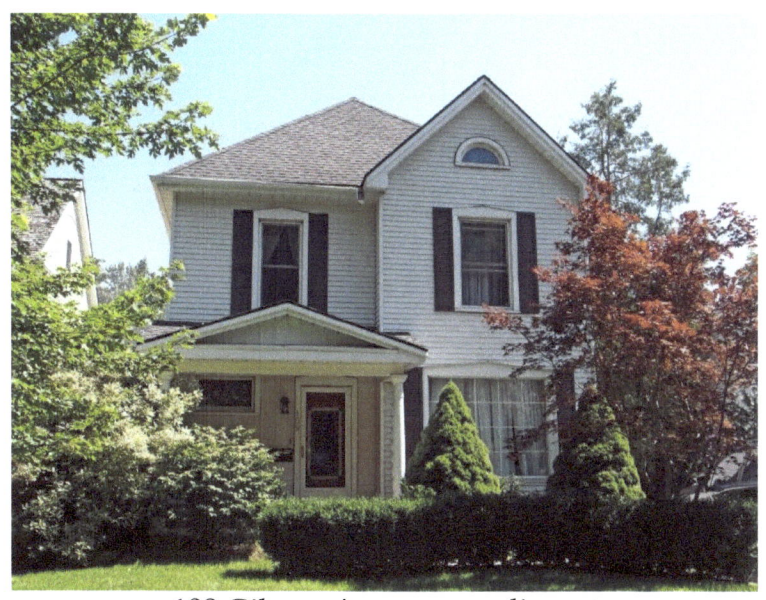

109 Gibson Avenue - pediment

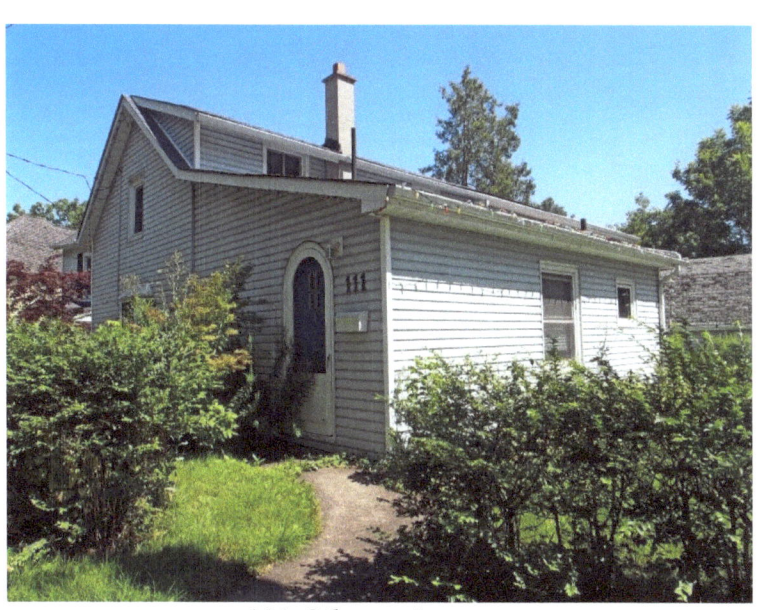

111 Gibson Avenue

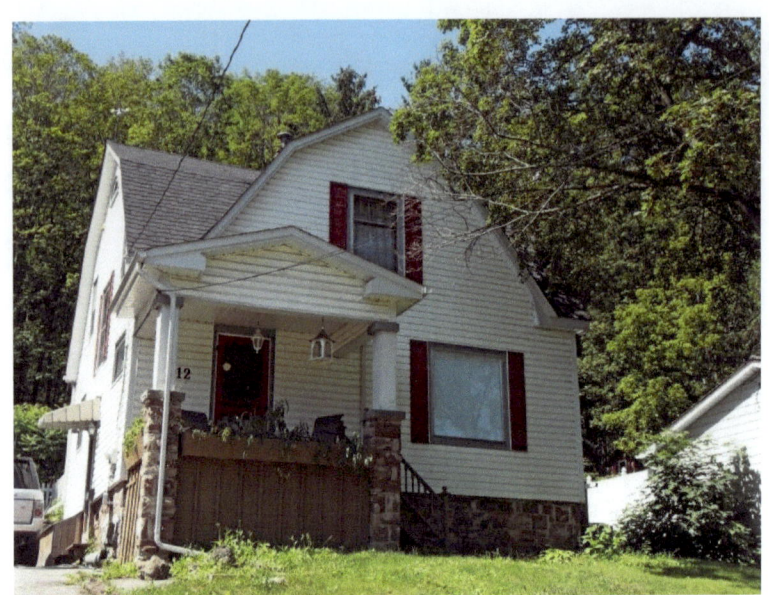

112 Gibson Avenue – Neo-Colonial – gambrel roof

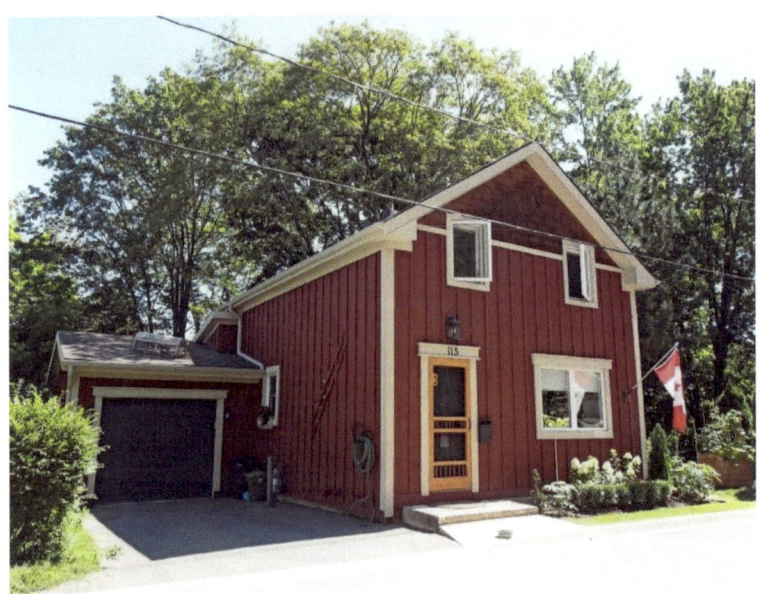

115 Gibson Avenue

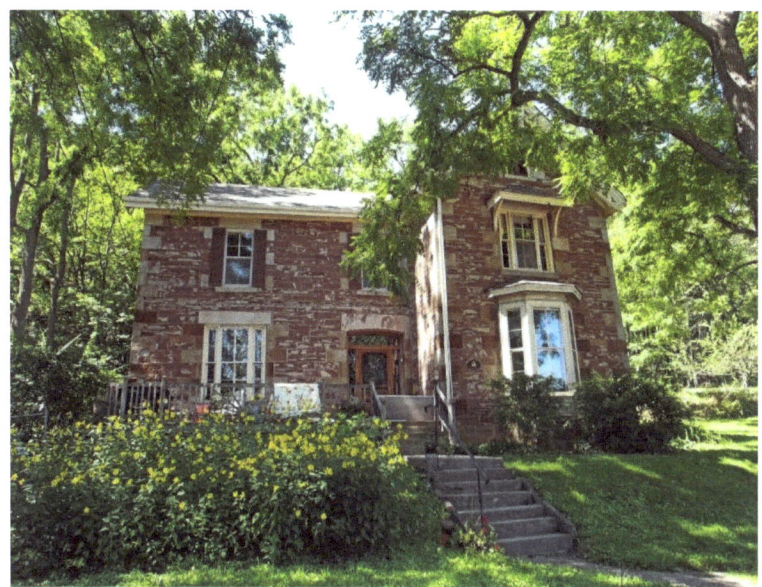

The Gibson house at 114 Gibson Avenue was built circa 1860 by Robert Lillie Gibson using red variegated free stone from his quarries on the escarpment above. He came to Grimsby in search of good stone for quarrying. Robert and the men in this family were stonemasons from Scotland. He settled on the west above Grimsby and established a quarry there. He met and fell in love with Frances Thompson and they were married. Robert built the little house at 102 Gibson Avenue for his bride, but he began work on the lovely stone house by Forty Mile Creek. Robert's quarry above the house was a success due to the building boom in public structures and railway bridges during that era. Rock was carried from the quarry to waiting ships by means of a little railway that ran from the base of the escarpment to the foot of Maple Avenue where a pier was built for this purpose.

In 1870, Robert opened a second quarry in Beamsville. At that time, he brought his 21-year-old nephew, William from Scotland to act as bookkeeper. When Robert died in an unfortunate accident in 1882, William took over the operation of the quarries.

In 1891, William ran successfully for Parliament, holding his seat until 1902. He was then appointed to the Senate. Senator Gibson School in Beamsville is named for him.

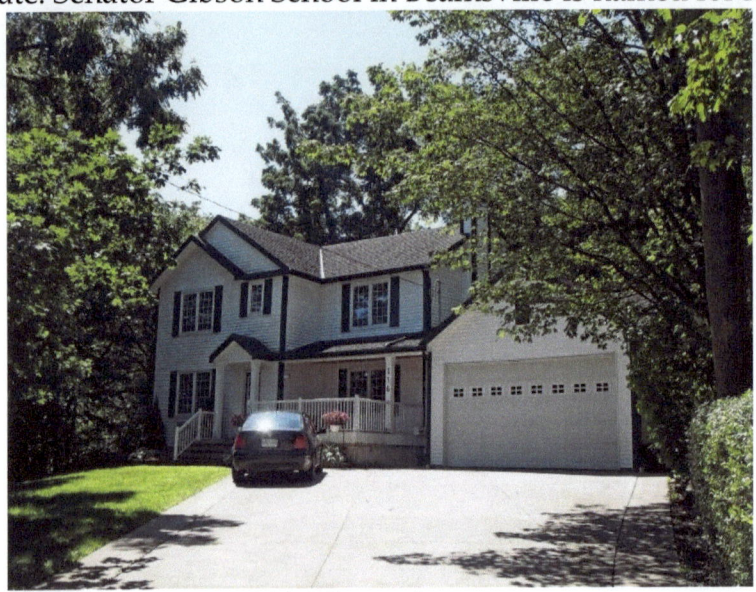

116 Gibson Avenue

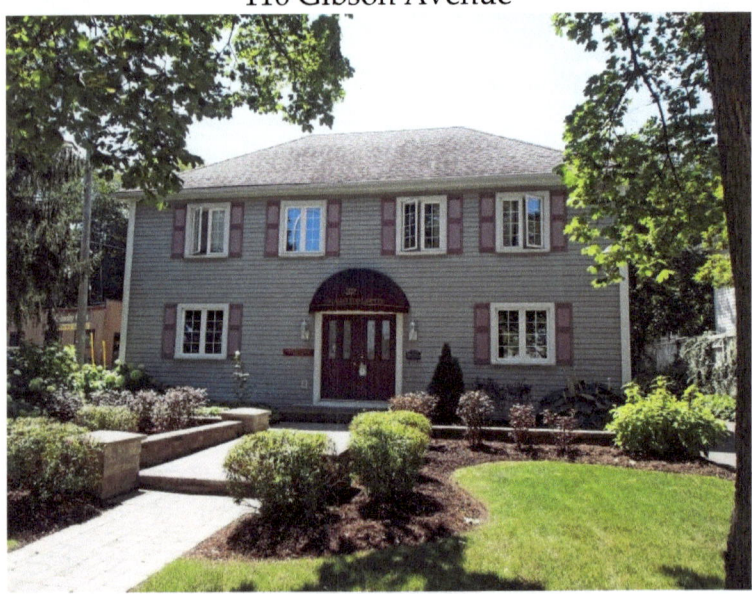

32 Elm Street – hipped roof, shutters

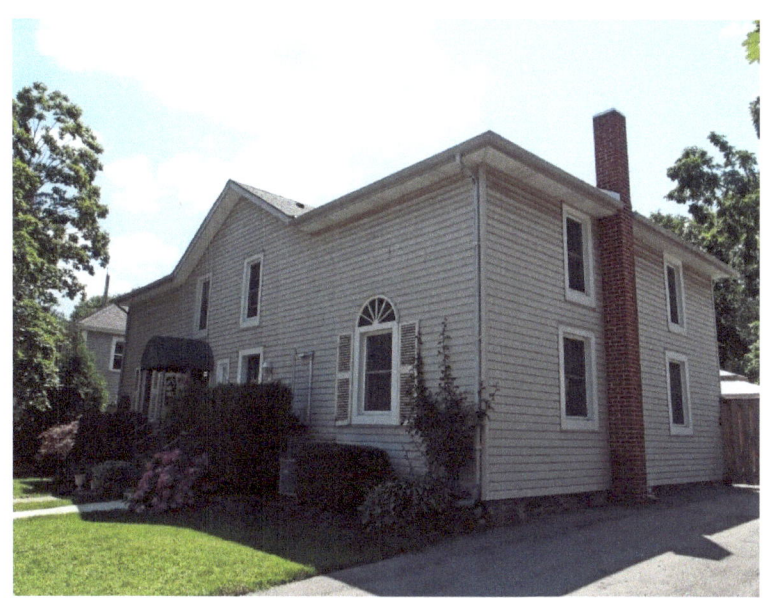

30 Elm Street

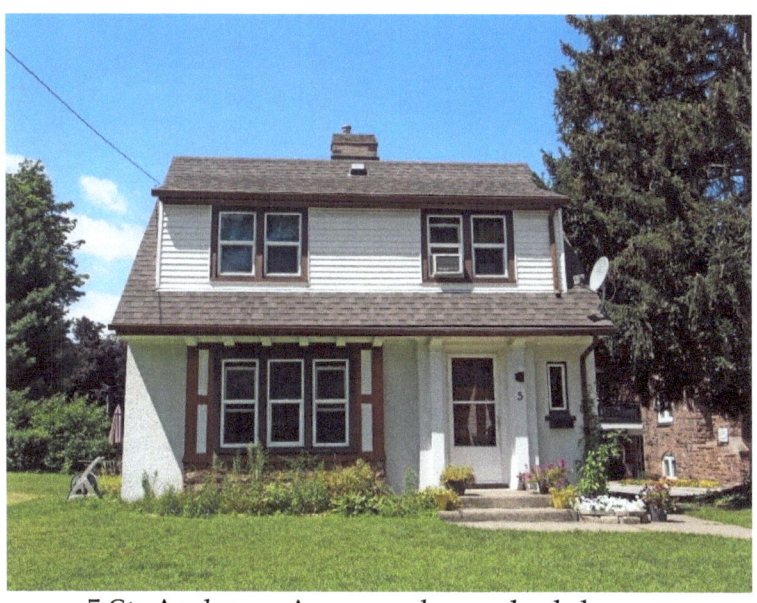

5 St. Andrews Avenue - large shed dormer

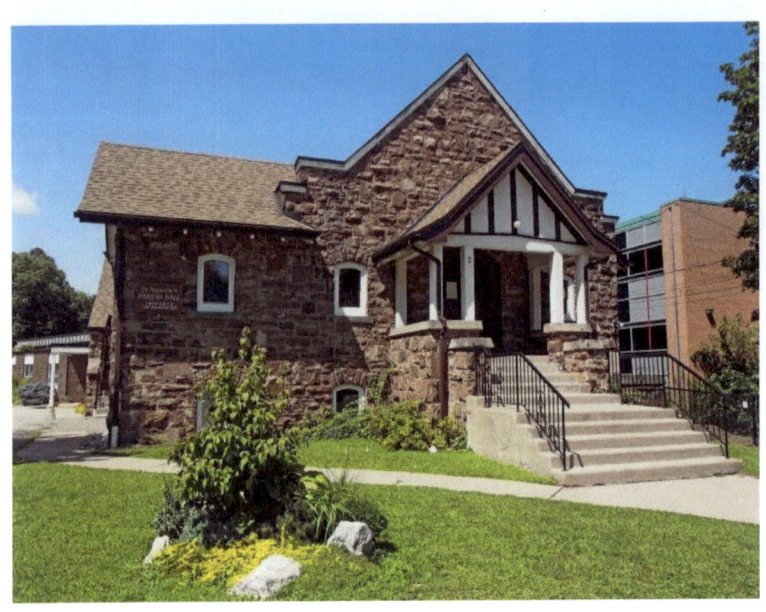

7 St. Andrews Avenue – St. Andrews Parish Hall - 1910

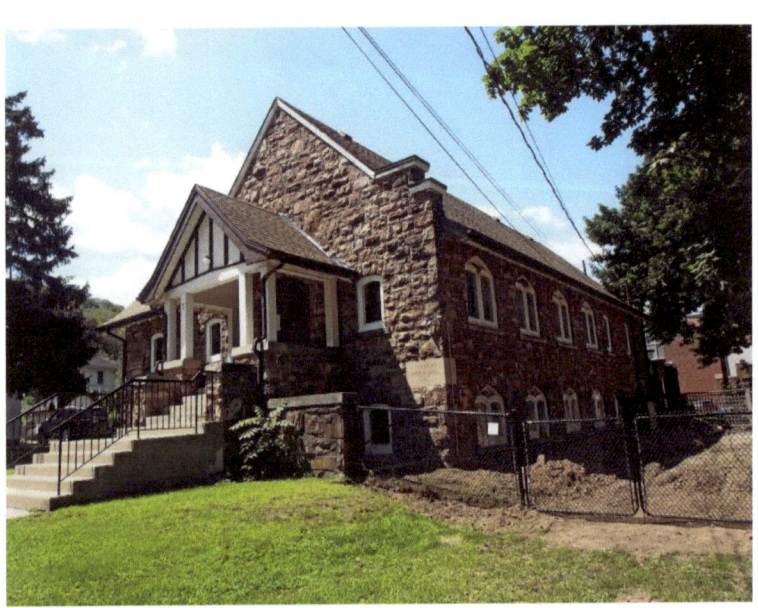

The present stone church was built in 1819.

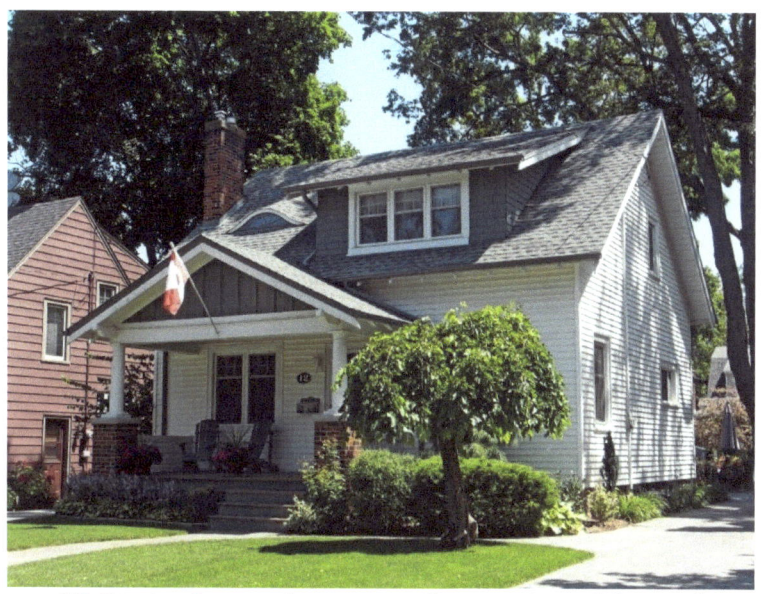

12 St. Andrews Avenue – dormer in gable roof

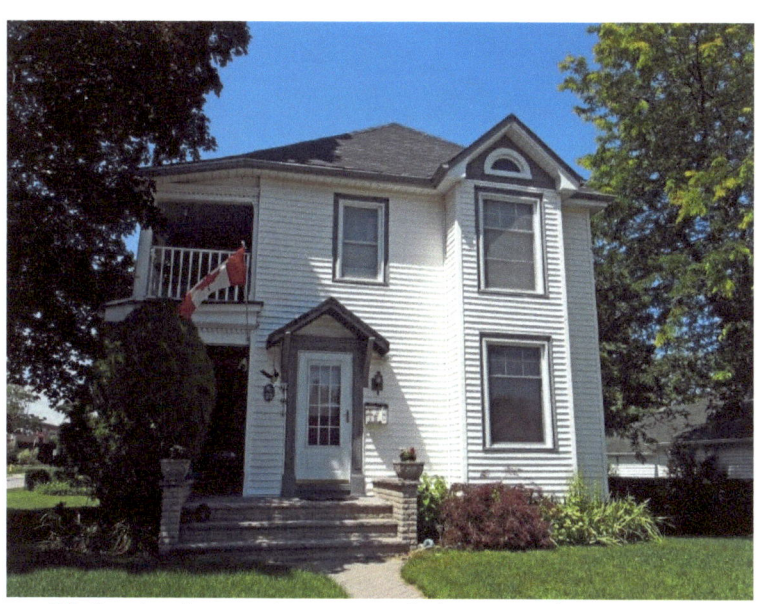

23 St. Andrews Avenue – 2½-storey frontispiece

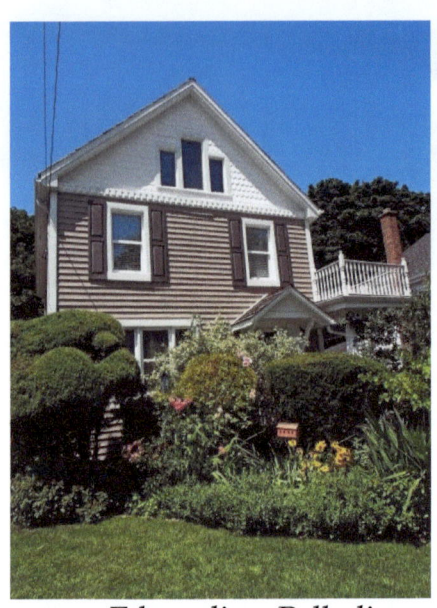

St. Andrews Avenue – Edwardian, Palladian window in gable

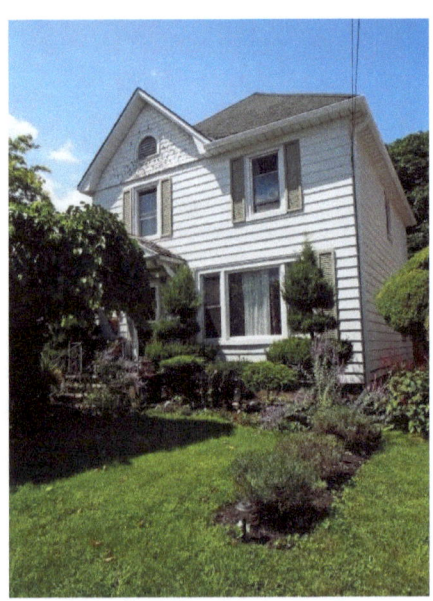

St. Andrews Avenue

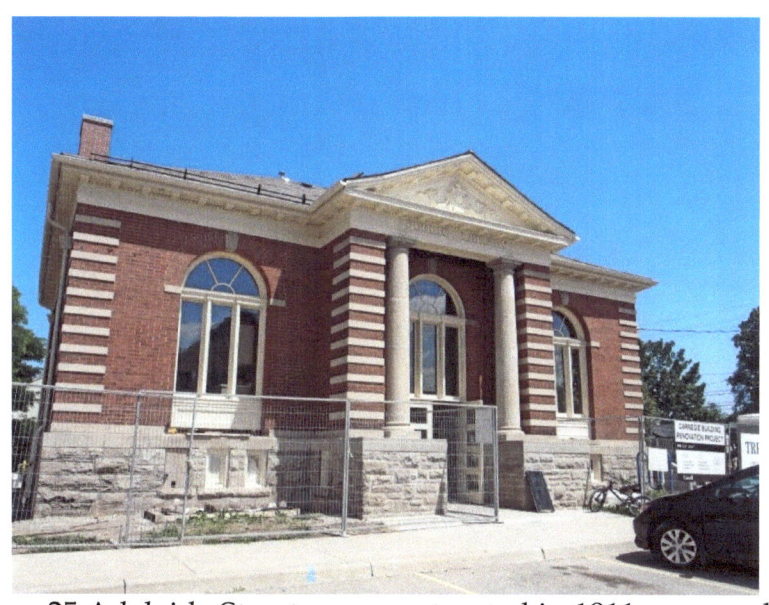

25 Adelaide Street was constructed in 1911 as a result of an $8,000 grant from the Carnegie Corporation of New York whose purpose was to promote the advancement of knowledge. It served as Grimsby's library until 2003. The three-part façade represents strength, wisdom and beauty. The portico is in the classic Greek design.

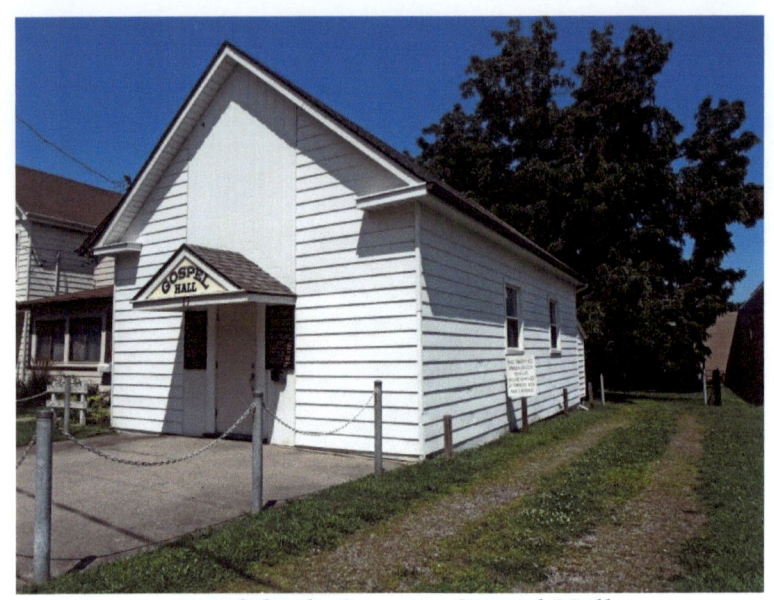
17 Adelaide Street – Gospel Hall

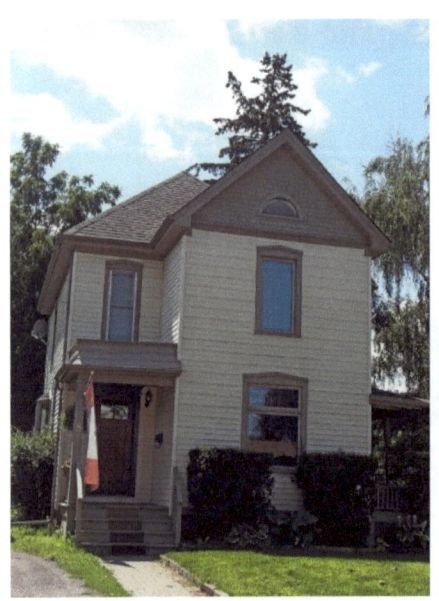
8 Adelaide Street

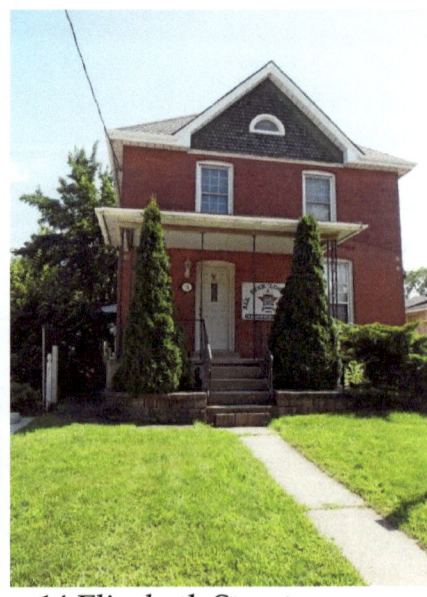
14 Elizabeth Street

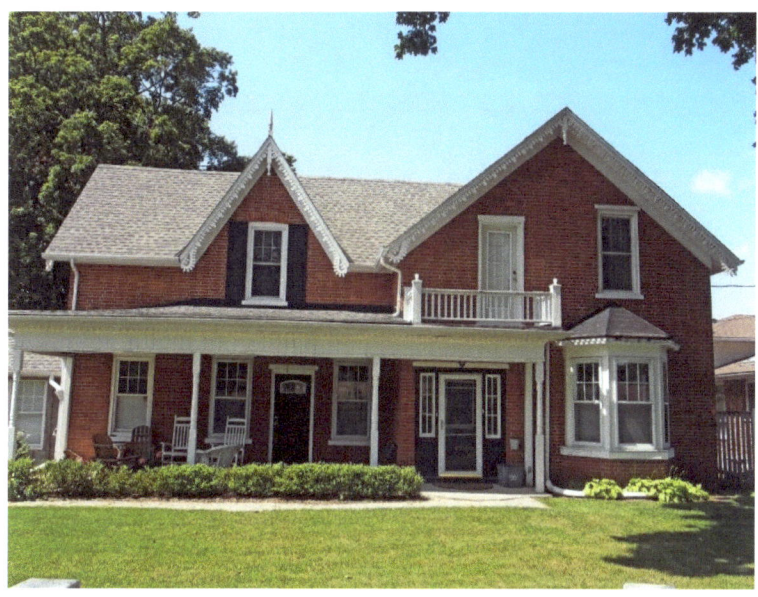

Elizabeth Street – Gothic Revival – verge board trim and finials on gables, second floor balcony, bay window

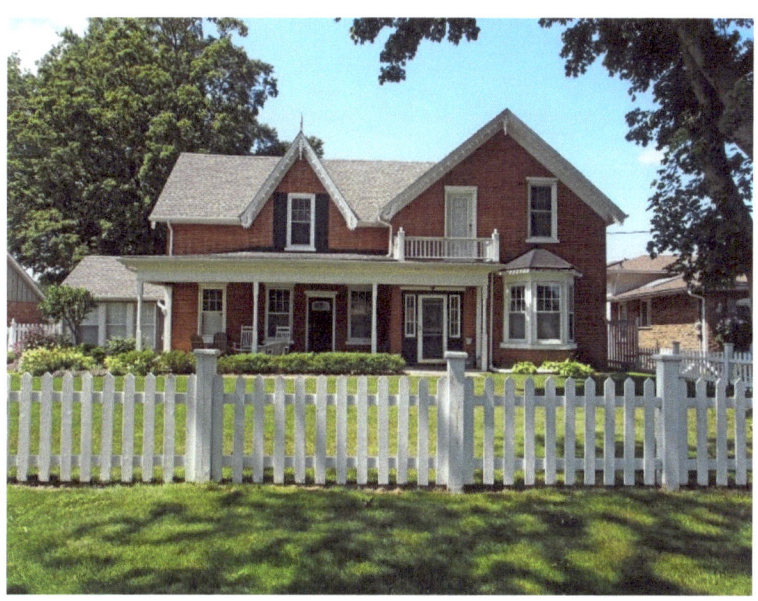

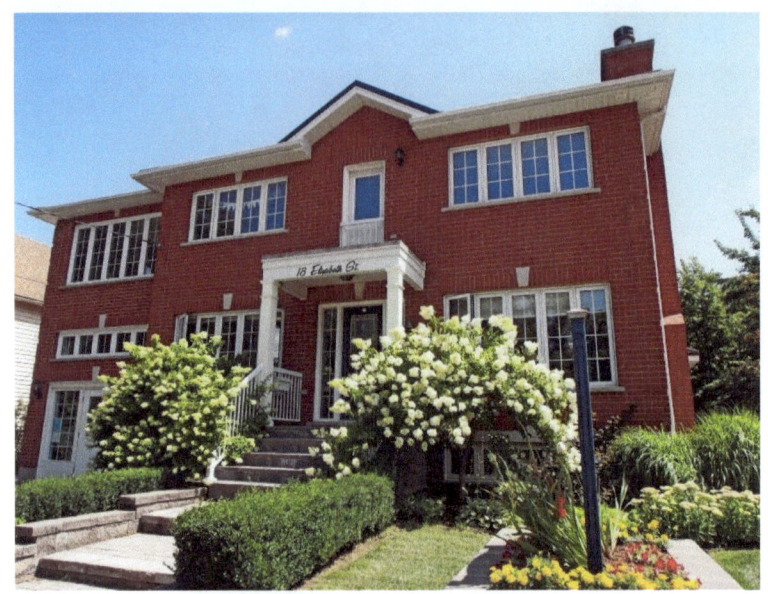

18 Elizabeth Street - Georgian

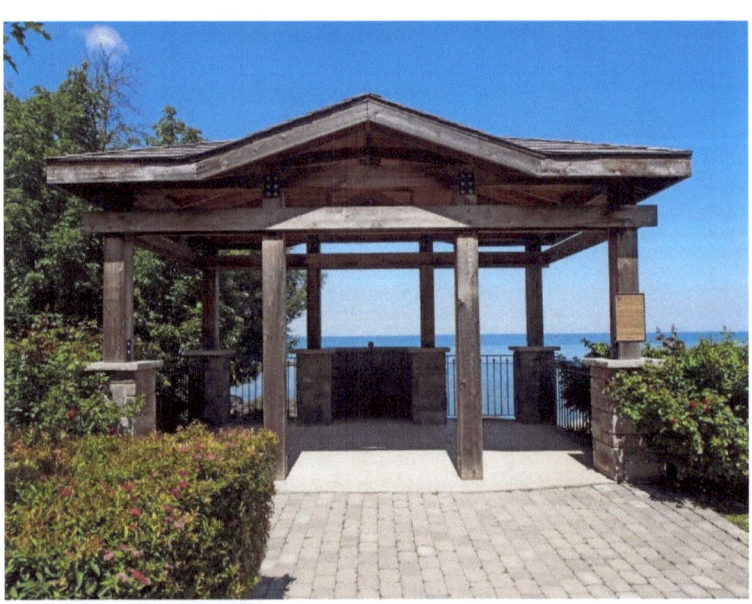

The gazebo was dedicated in commemoration of 200 years of peace between Canada and the United States.

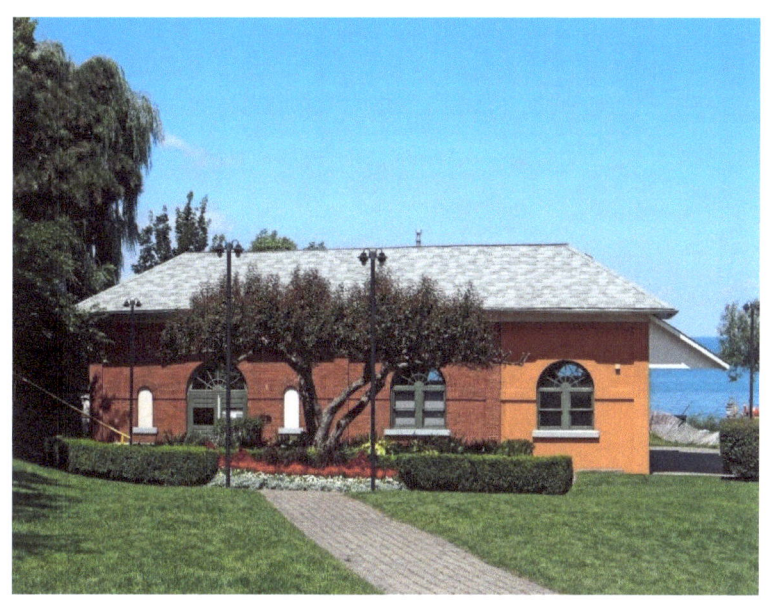

Elizabeth Street - Pump House – 1905 to the 1990s

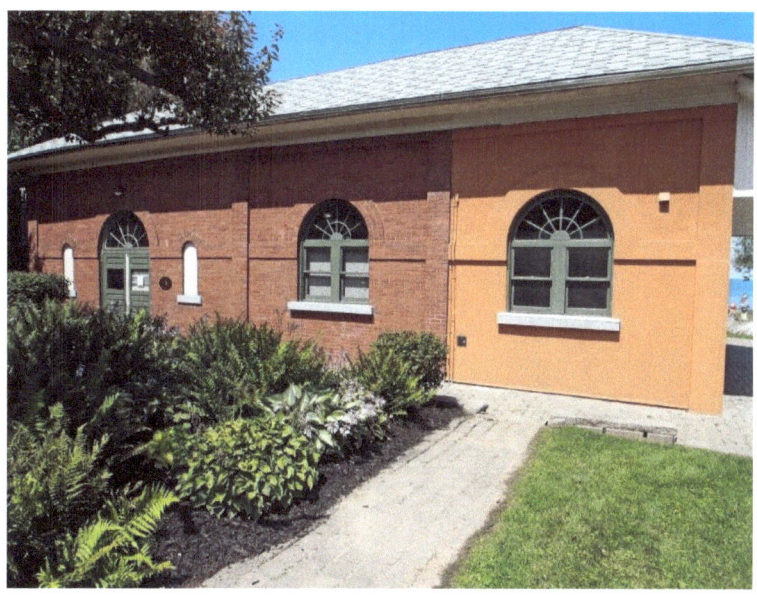

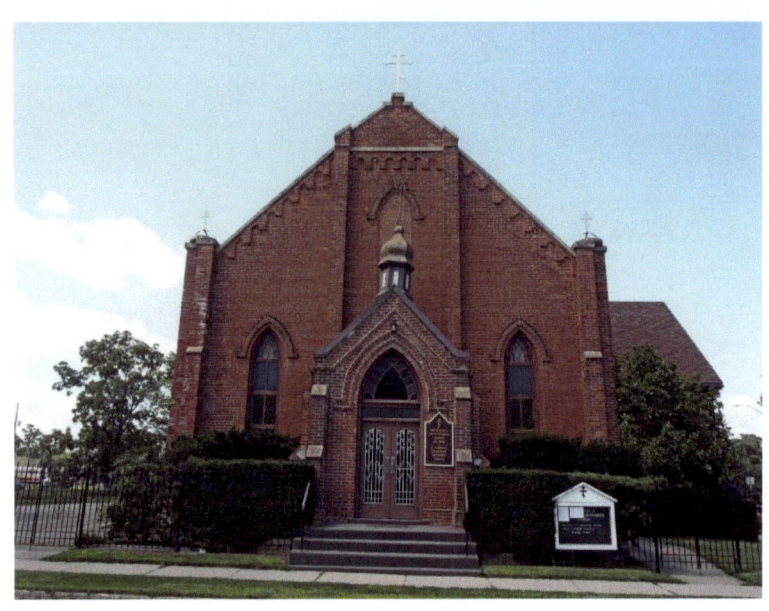

439 Elizabeth Street – St. George's Ukrainian Orthodox Church

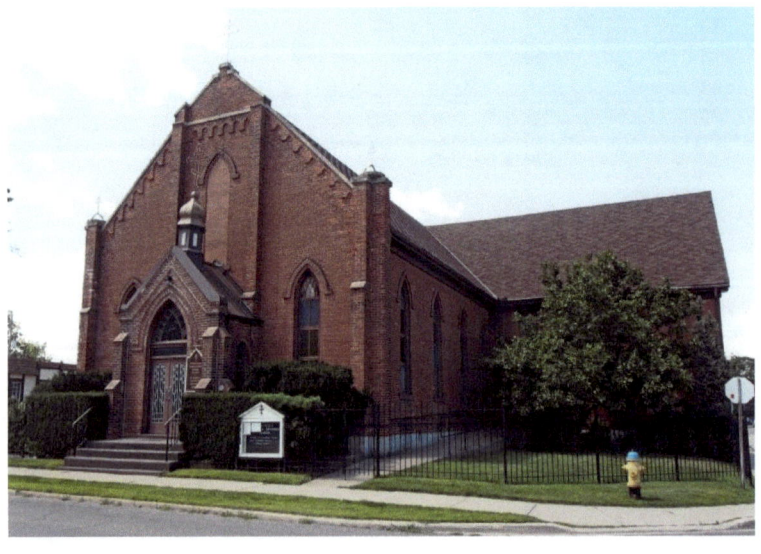

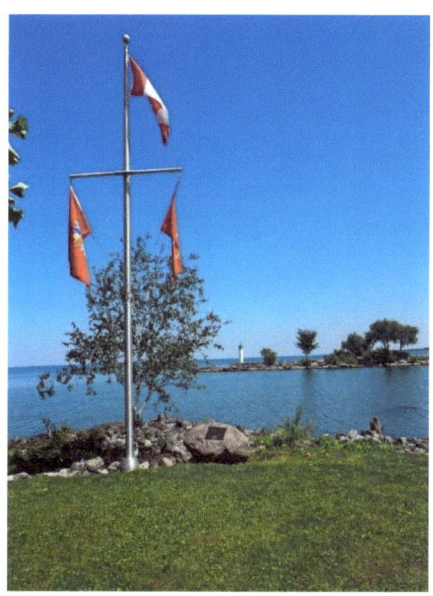

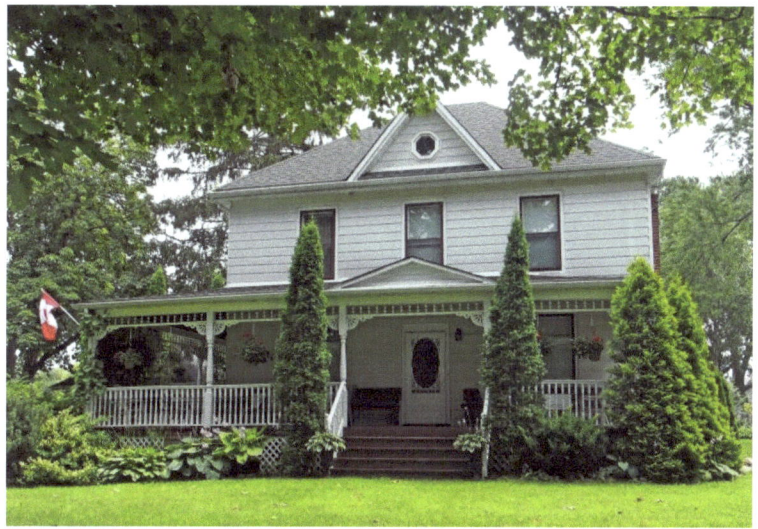

18 Nelles Road North – William Boise Nelles built this house on his fruit farm in 1905. Around 1800, William Nelles built The Hermitage on land near Lake Ontario. When he died, the land was divided between his sons, Peter Ball Nelles and John Adolphus Nelles. Peter had the eastern portion of the land, which he called Chestnut Park. John Adolphus had the western part on which he built Lakelawn.

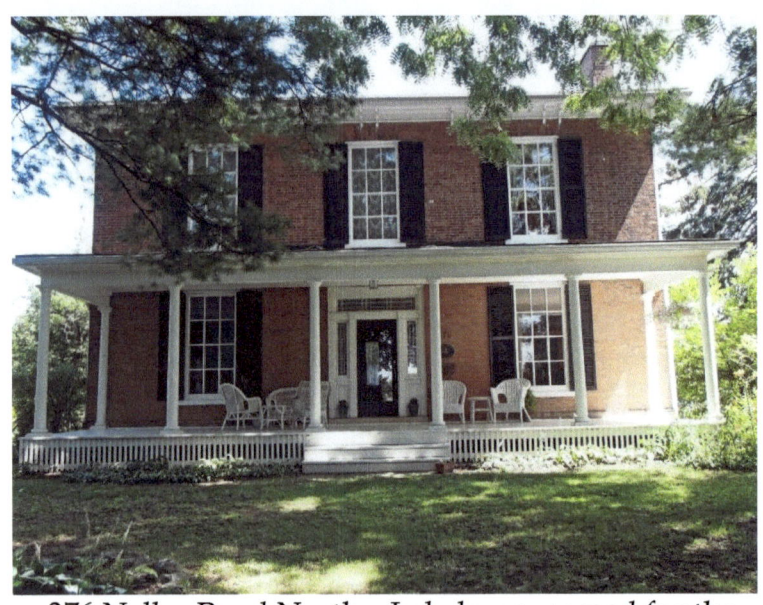

376 Nelles Road North – Lakelawn, named for the grassy stretch between the house and lake, was built in 1846 by John Adolphus Nelles, son of William and nephew of Robert. The house remained in the family until the death of John's great-granddaughter, Mary Burnham in 1986.

John's brother Peter Ball Nelles shared this property and built a lovely home called Stone Shanty. It was unfortunately razed when the Queen Elizabeth Highway was built.

At one time, Lake Street was part of the military road which ran along the lakeshore.

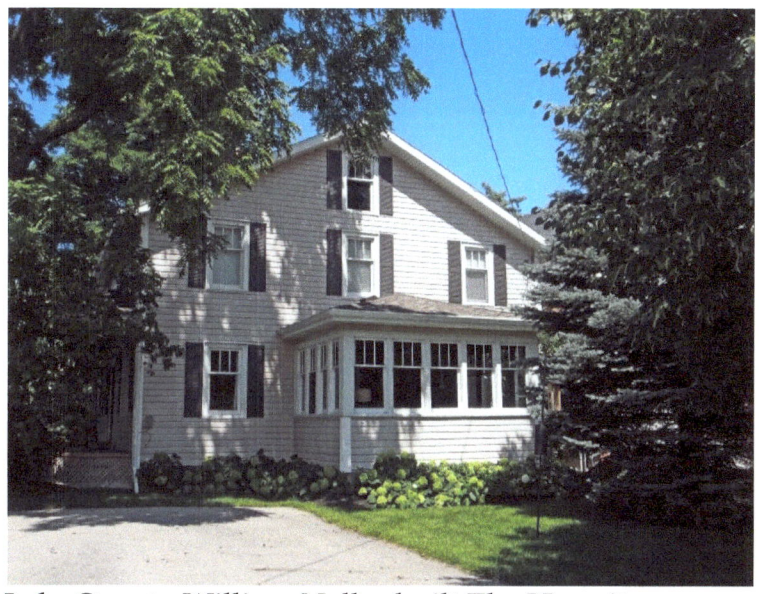

139 Lake Street - William Nelles built The Hermitage around 1800. This house played an interesting part in the War 1812. American prisoners were housed in the barn after the Engagement at the Forty.

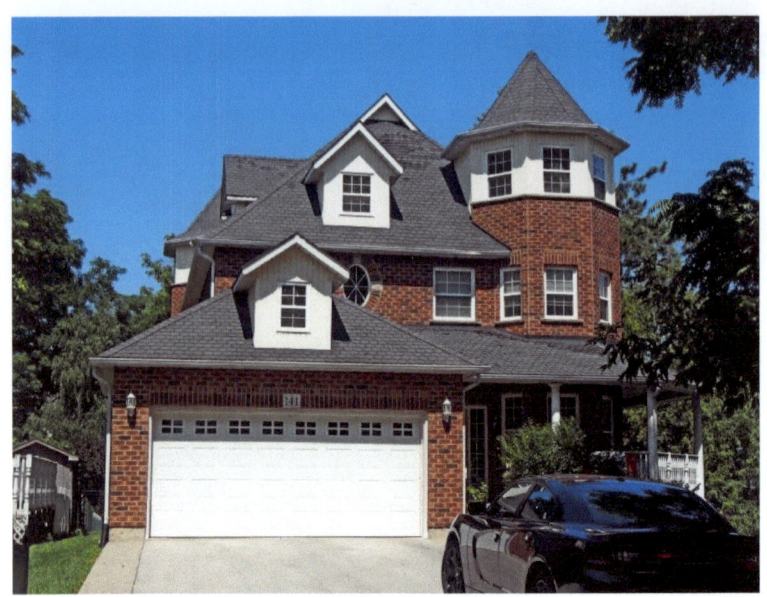

141 Lake Street – Queen Anne style – three-storey tower, dormers

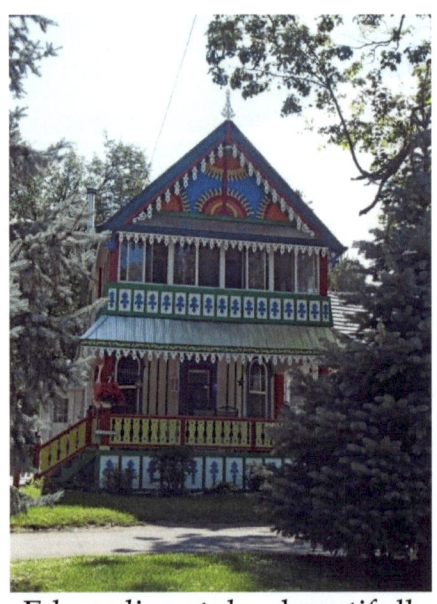

Lake Street – Edwardian style – beautifully colored and decorated

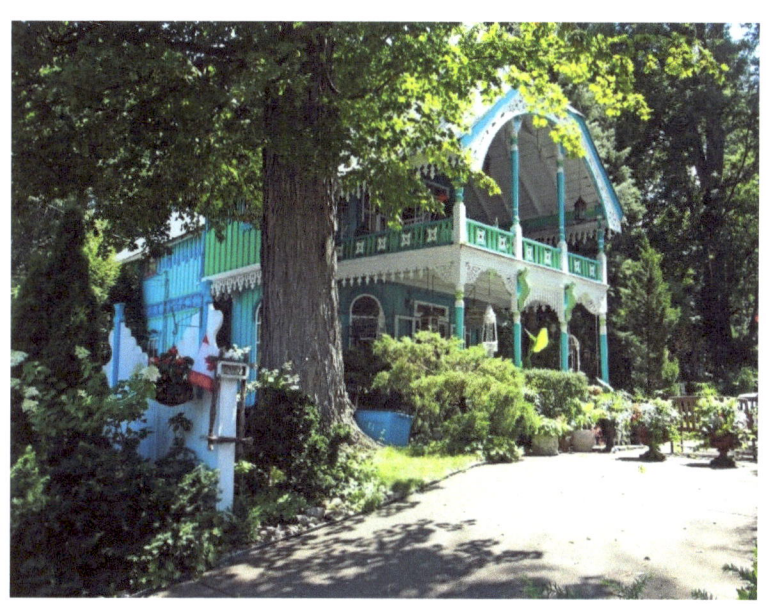

252 Lake Street - Ledingham Cottage

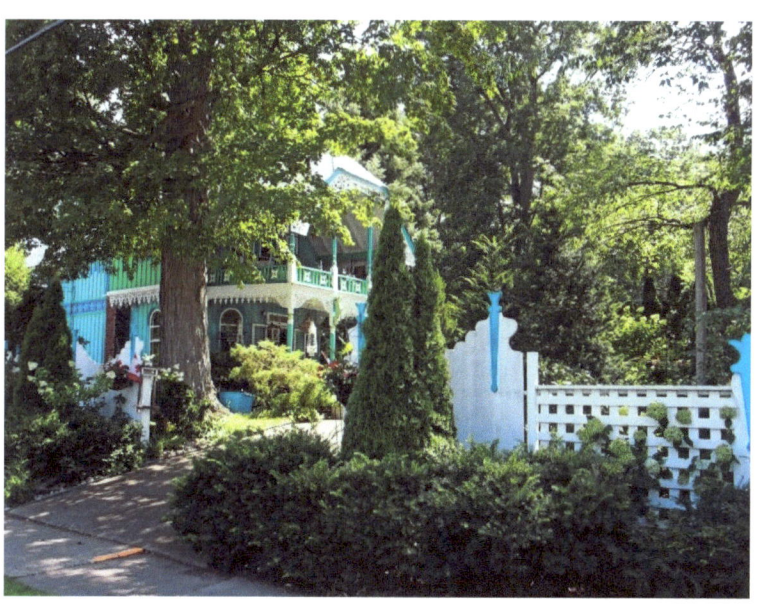

In 1846, John Beamer Bowslaugh, a devout Methodist, offered the use of a grove along the shores of Lake Ontario, for a giant temperance meeting. In 1859, a summer revival took place and they carried this tradition on for 16 years, except in 1862.

In 1874, Noah Phelps had a dream of building a community modelled on the new Methodist Camp at Chautauqua, New York. By 1875, John Bowslaugh deeded 12.5 acres to the Methodists. The Ontario Methodist Camp Ground Company was established with Noah Phelps as the first president. Fifty cottages were built close together on the original tent sites and were adorned with fretwork. Many cottages were built by Edward Bowslaugh (brother of John Bowslaugh). Typically, they were 1.5 stories, many with small balconies off the bedrooms on the second floor, just like Ledingham Cottage which was built in 1879 by Reverend Gallagher. The cottage received its name from the Ledingham family who lived there the longest and were the last to occupy it as a summer residence. Over time, the surrounding Methodist Camp evolved into an amusement park which eventually faded away, and the summer cottages became permanent year-round homes.

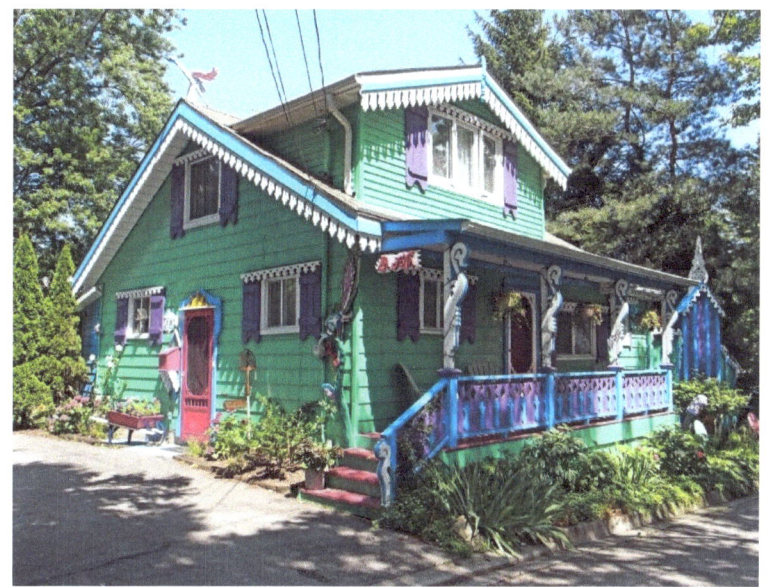

Fair Avenue – pastel colours, verge board trim on gables

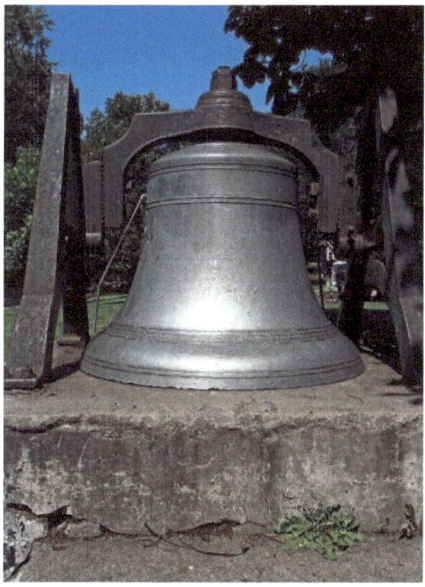

Bell Park

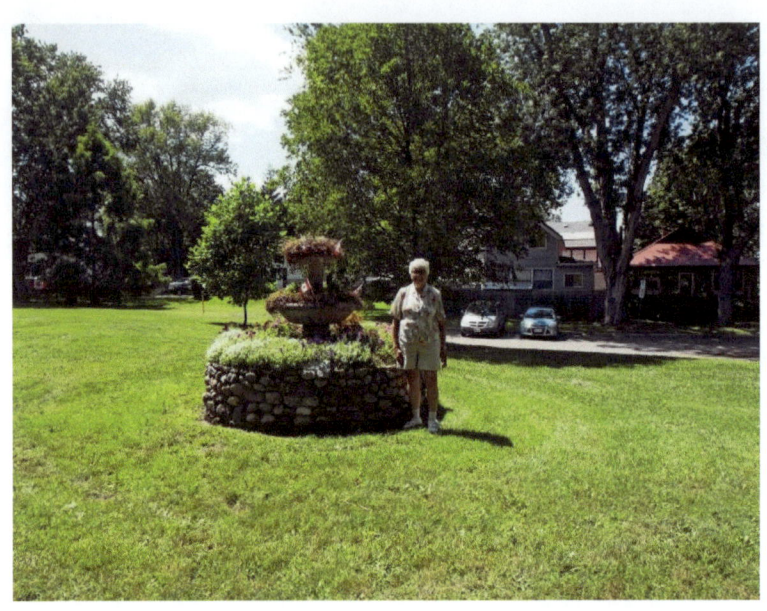

Bell Park is surrounded by some of the original cottages.

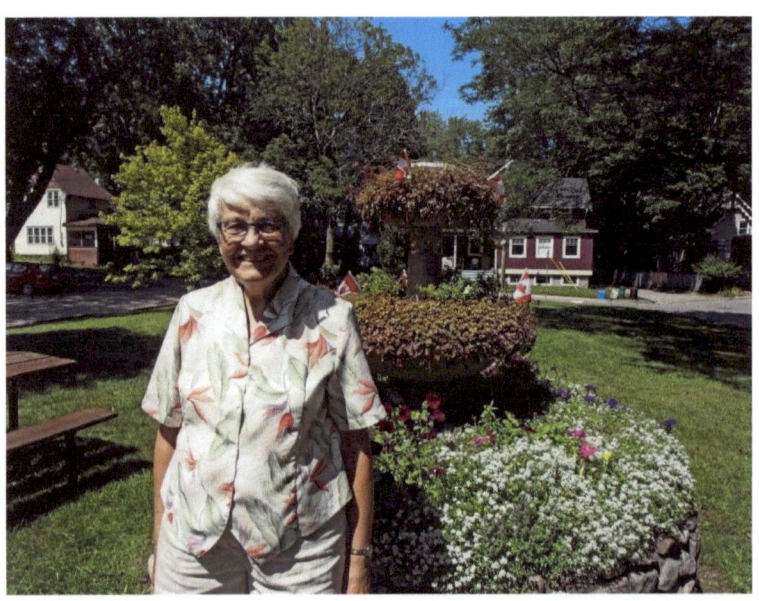

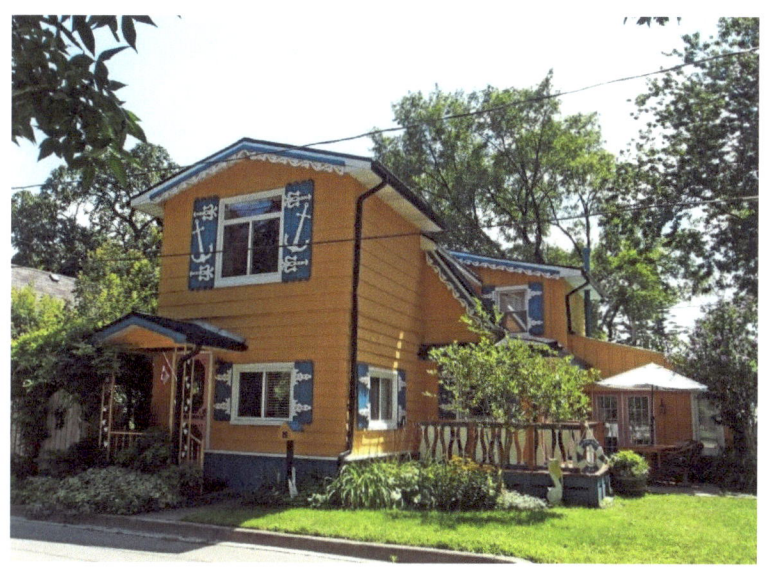

19 Fair Avenue

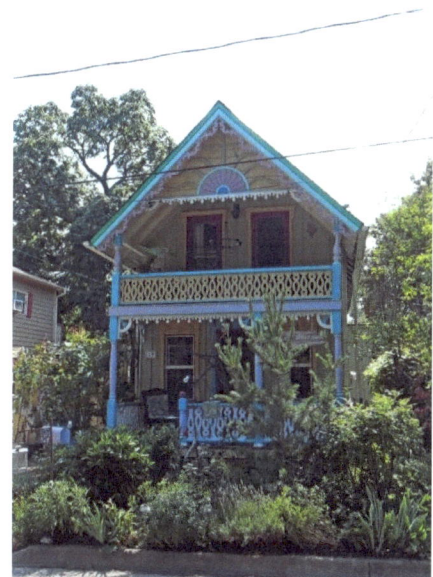

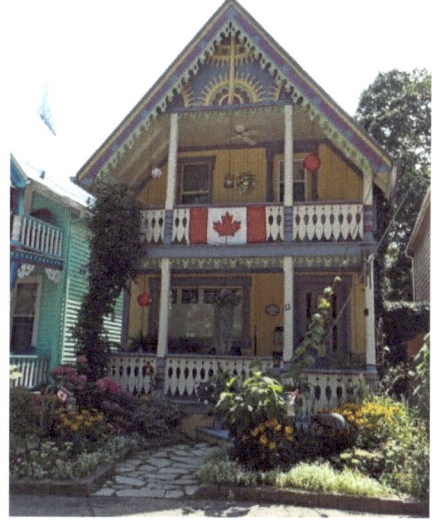

17 Fair Avenue       13 Fair Avenue
Edwardian style – second floor sleeping balconies

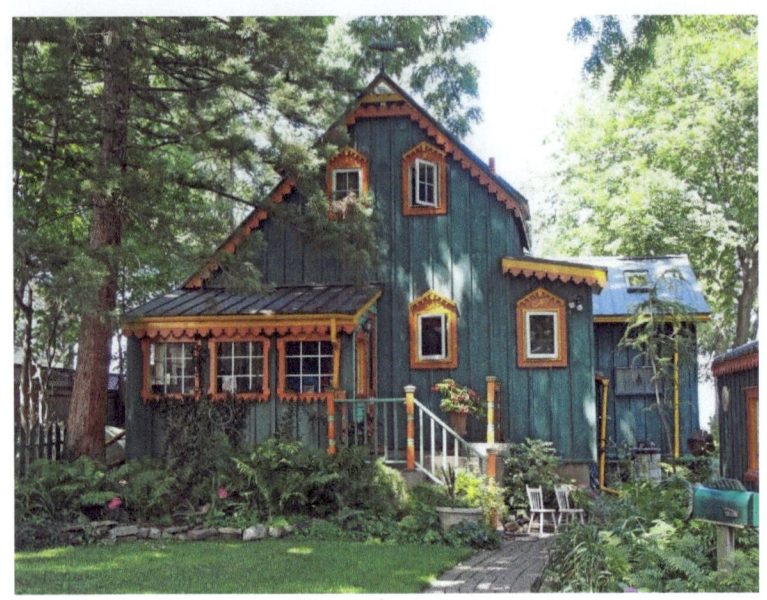

Temple Lane

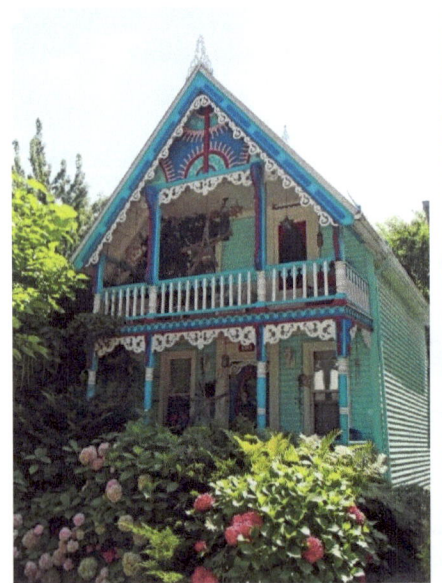 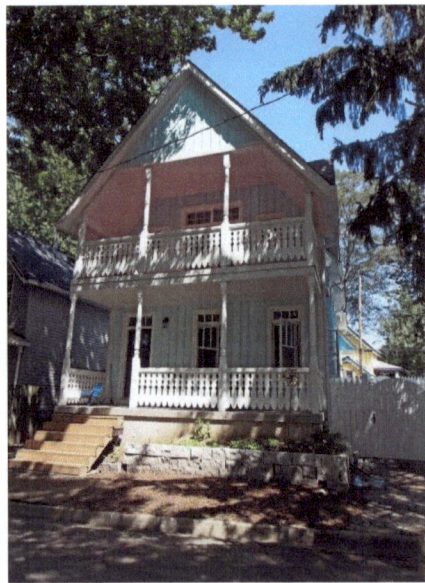

11 Fair Avenue          Third Street
Edwardian style – second floor sleeping balconies

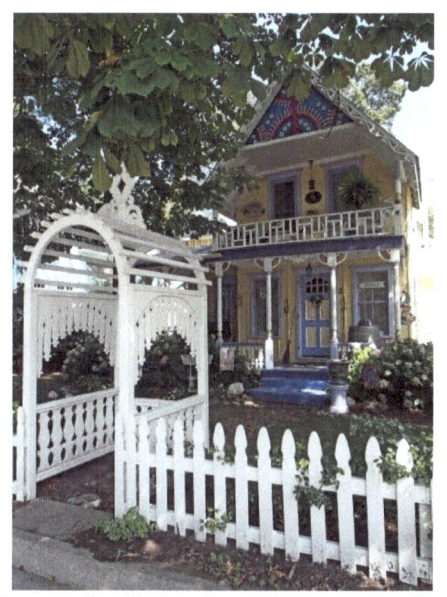

2 Third Street, built in the 1870s at the height of Grimsby Park's Chautauqua era, this board and batten cottage may have been the home and portrait studio of famous photographer J.H. Ford. The original cottage was extremely ornate with plenty of gingerbread trim, two upstairs porches, and ten doors! These cottage homes are all that remain from the original Grimsby Park.

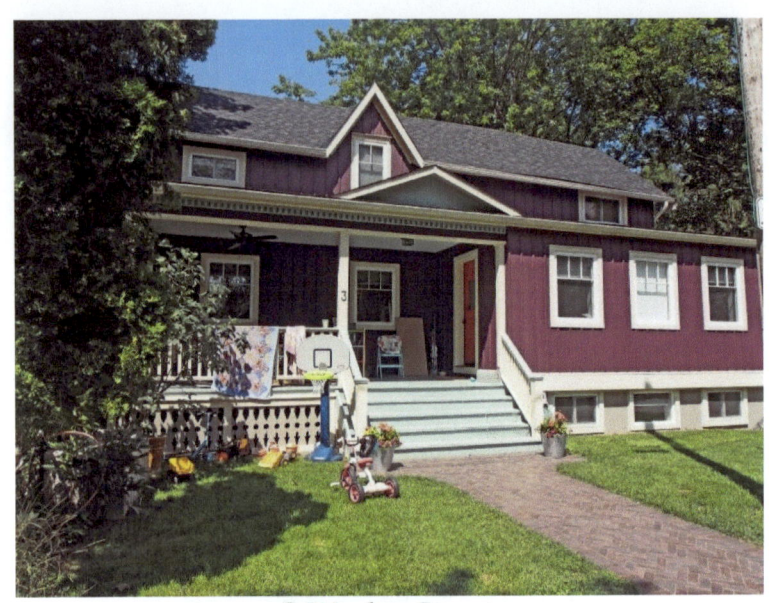

3 Wesley Street

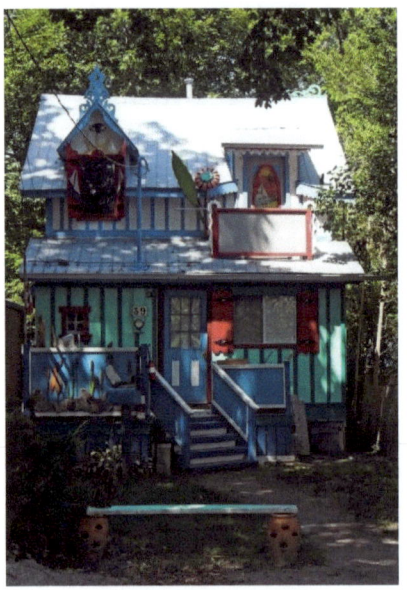

39 Wesley Street

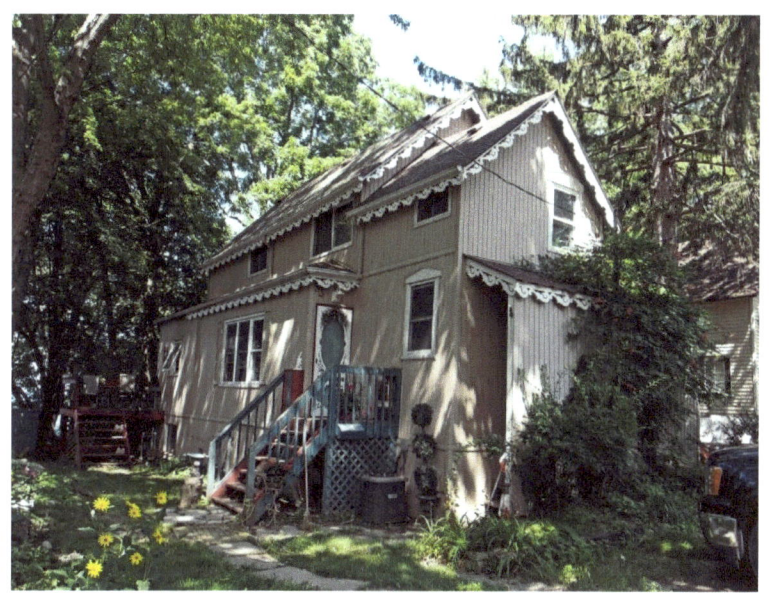

33 East Street

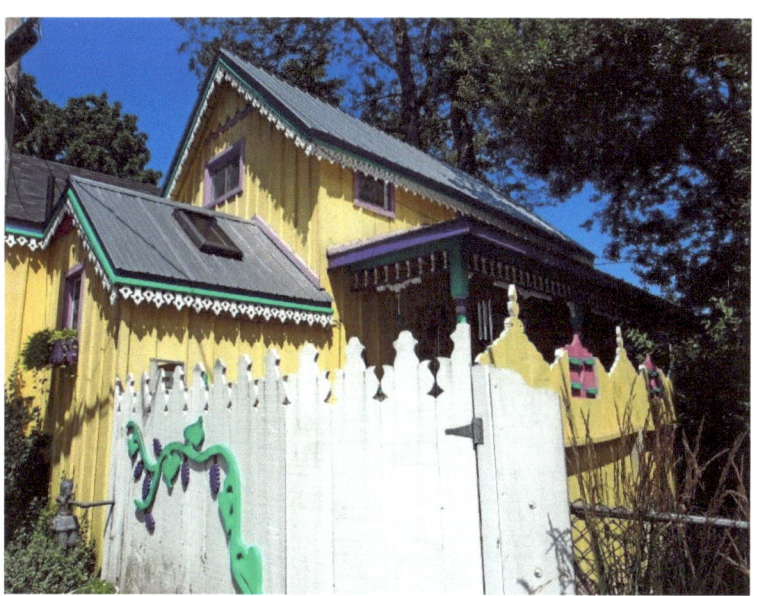

East Street

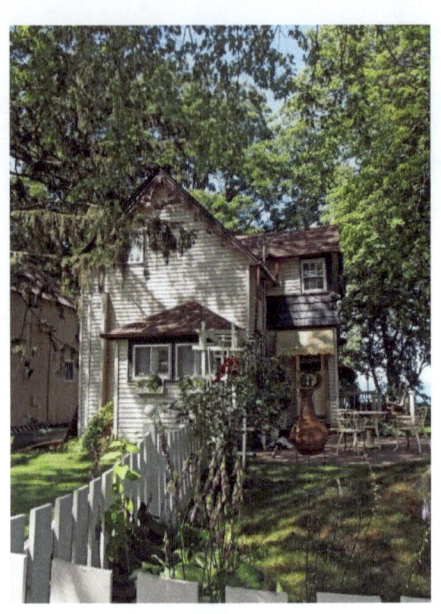

East Street

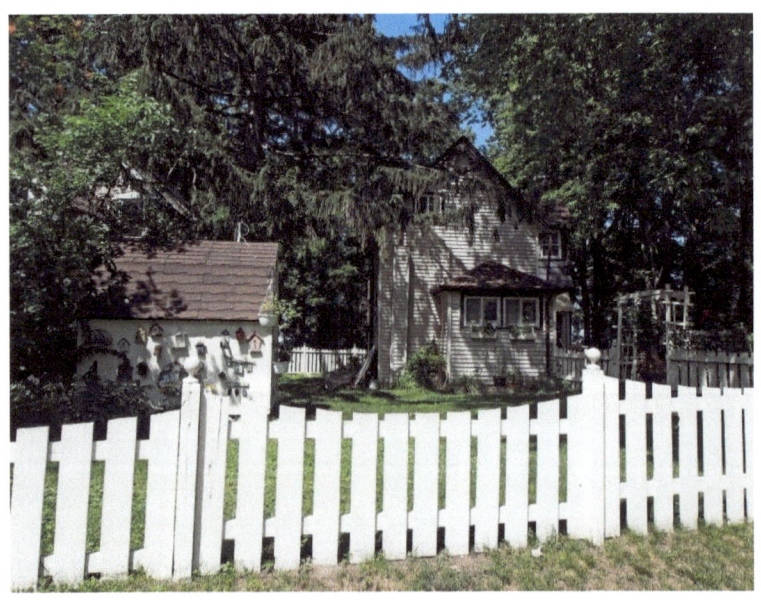

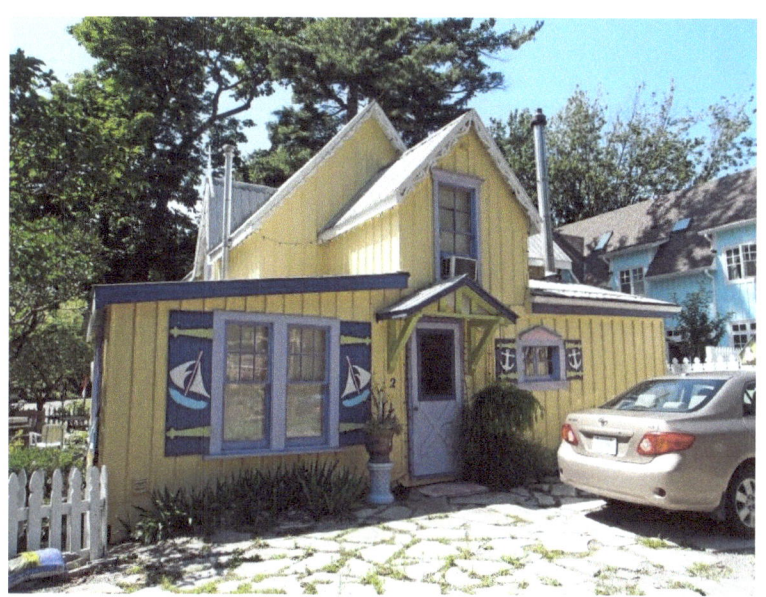

2 East Street

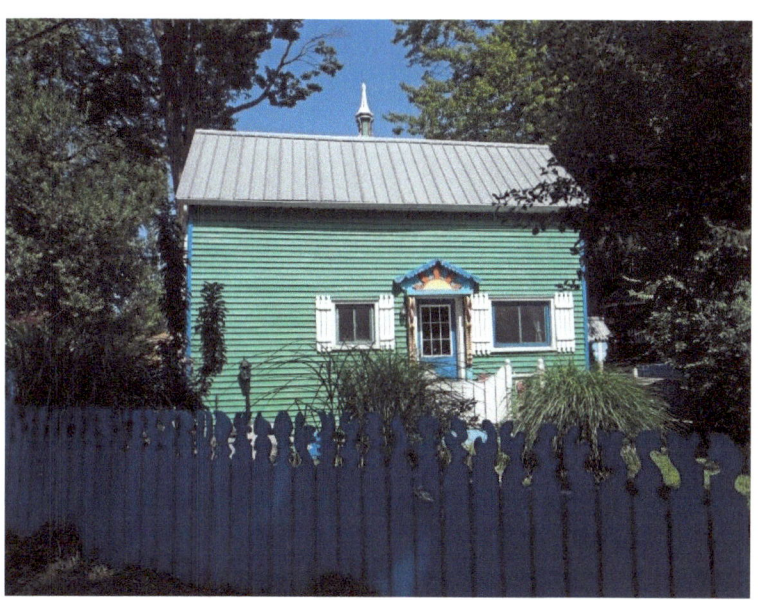

Colourful cupola on top

## Architectural Terms

| | |
|---|---|
| **Bay Window:** A window that projects out from a wall, in a semicircular, rectangular, or polygonal design. Used frequently in Gothic and Victorian designs.<br>Example: Elizabeth Street, Page 37 | 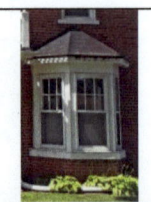 |
| **Buttress**: a masonry structure built against or projecting from a wall which serves to support or reinforce the wall. In Canadian architecture, they are sometimes used for decoration.<br>Example: 10 Mountain Street, Page 9 | 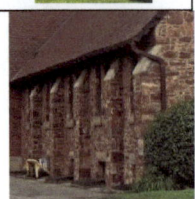 |
| **Capital:** The uppermost finish or decoration on a column. A Doric column is characterized by a plain column with no base, a shaft with twenty flutings, and a simple capital with a simple entablature.<br>Example: 25 Adelaide Street, Page 35 | 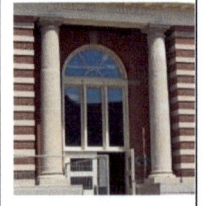 |
| **Cornice Return:** decorative element on the end of a gable.<br><br>Example: 102 Gibson Avenue, Page 25 | 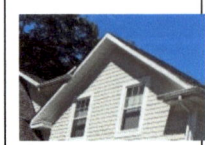 |
| **Cupola:** A domed or curved roof rising from a building as a decorative element.<br><br>Example: East Street, Page 55 | 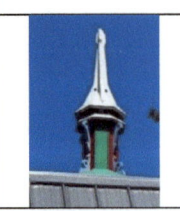 |
| **Dichromatic brickwork**: the use of two colours of brick, tile or slate to decorate a façade.<br><br>Example: 103 Mountain Road, Page 6 | 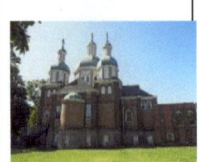 |

| | |
|---|---|
| **Dormer**: (French for "sleep") a gable end window that pierces through the plane of a sloping roof surface to create usable space in the top floor or attic of a building by adding headroom.<br>Example: Mountain Street, Page 16 | 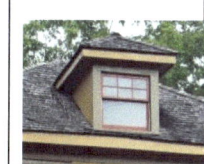 |
| **Frontispiece:** a portion of the façade of a building, usually a centred doorway that is slightly raised from the rest of the building, usually has extensive ornamentation. Frontispieces are usually Classical in design with white columned porches.<br>Example: 23 St. Andrews Avenue, Page 33 | 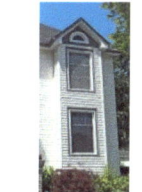 |
| **Gable**: the triangular portion of a wall between the edges of a sloping roof.<br>Example: 107 Gibson Avenue, Page 26 | 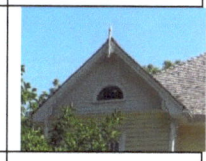 |
| **Gambrel Roof**: a symmetrical two-sided roof with two slopes on each side; the upper slope is positioned at a shallow angle, while the lower slope is steep. It is similar to a mansard roof, but a gambrel has vertical gable ends instead of being hipped at the four corners of the building.<br>Example: 11 Nelles Boulevard, Page 21 | 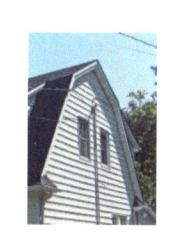 |
| **Hipped Roof**: a roof where all sides slope downwards to the walls with no gables.<br>Example: 32 Elm Street, Page 30 | 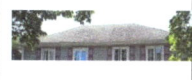 |
| **Oriel Window** - These small areas were originally set into walls and galleries for the purpose of private prayer. Over time, any projecting window or area on an upper floor was called an oriel.<br>Example: Robinson Street South, Page 8 | 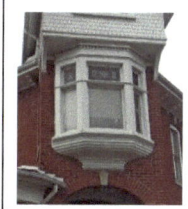 |

| | |
|---|---|
| **Palladian Window**: a large window that is divided into three sections with the centre section larger than the two side sections and usually arched.<br>Example: 19 Mountain Street, Page 13 | |
| **Pediment**: a triangular section above the door or portico, usually supported by columns. The inside of the triangle is called the tympanum.<br>Example: 25 Adelaide Street, Page 35 | |
| **Quoin**: masonry blocks at the corner of a wall, often a decorative feature, usually larger or of a different colour than the rest of the wall.<br><br>Example: 7 Murray Street, Page 17 | |
| **Rose Window:** a circular window with ornamental tracery radiating from the centre.<br><br><br>Example: 19 Elm Street, Page 11 | |
| **Sidelight**: a vertical window that flanks a door, and is often used to emphasize the importance of a primary entrance.<br><br>Example: 22 Nelles Boulevard, Page 18 | |

| | |
|---|---|
| **Tower:** A circular, square, or octagonal vertical structure higher than the surrounding structure that is usually part of an existing building and is created either for extra defense or for a specific purpose such as a clock or a bell tower.<br><br>Example: 141 Lake Street, Page 44 | 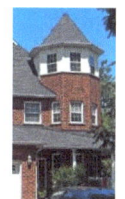 |
| **Transom Window:** the light above the doorway, also called a fanlight.<br><br>Example: 25 Adelaide Street, Page 35 | 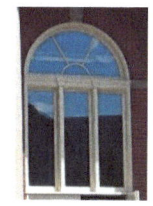 |
| **Verge board and Finial**: also called bargeboards – hang from the projecting end of a roof and are often elaborately carved and ornamented. **Finial:** ornament added to the top of a gable, pinnacle, canopy or spire – a Gothic element.<br>Example: Elizabeth Street, Page 37 | 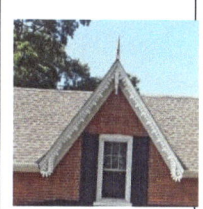 |

Building Styles

| | |
|---|---|
| **Edwardian**, 1900-1930 – This style bridges the ornate and elaborate styles of the Victorian era and the simplified styles of the 20th century. Edwardian Classicism provided simple, balanced facades, simple rooflines, dormer windows, large front porches, and smooth brick surfaces. Voussoirs and keystones are used sparingly and are understated. Finials and cresting are absent. Cornice brackets and braces are block-like and openings have flat arches or plain stone lintels.<br>Example: 11 Fair Avenue, Page 50 | 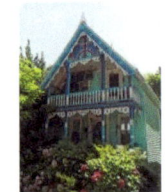 |
| **Georgian**, before 1860 – This style began with the British King Georges in the 18th century. These buildings have balanced facades around a central door, medium-pitched gable roofs, and small paned windows.<br>Example: 14 Robinson Street South, Page 7 | 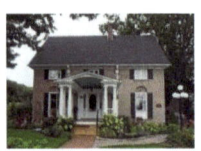 |
| **Gothic Revival**, 1830-1890 – These decorative buildings have sharply-pitched gables with highly detailed verge boards, pointed-arch window openings, and dichromatic brickwork. It is a common style in Ontario.<br>Example: 29 Mountain Street, Page 15 | 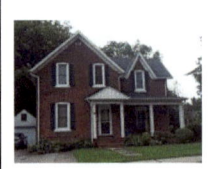 |

| | |
|---|---|
| **Greek Revival** – have gabled or hipped roofs with low pitches. The cornice of the main roof usually has a wide band which represents the entablature of classical Greek architecture consisting of the frieze and the architrave. Greek or Roman columns usually support the porch. The front door is surrounded by sidelights and a rectangular transom and is usually dressed with pilasters, pediments and/or columns.<br>Example: 25 Adelaide Street, Page 35 | 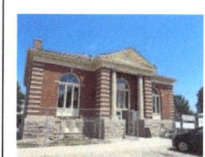 |
| **Neo-Classical,** 1810-1850 – This style was a direct result of the War of 1812. Many Upper Canadians returning from the war with the United States were second or third generation Loyalists who had inherited land and means from their forefathers. Once the conflict had passed, they had the money and the time to expand their holdings and indulge their architectural whims. Both residential and commercial buildings were constructed on the traditional Georgian plan, but they had a new gaiety and light-heartedness. Detailing became more refined, delicate, and elegant.<br>Example: 14 Robinson Street South, Page 7 - portico | 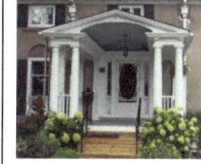 |

| | |
|---|---|
| **Neo-colonial** (also Colonial Revival, Georgian Revival or Neo-Georgian) architecture seeks to revive elements of architectural style of American colonial architecture of the period around the Revolutionary War which drew strongly from Georgian architecture of Great Britain. Architecture from the 18th and early 19th centuries in Ontario includes a wide assortment of detailing and ornament applied to a design centered around the fireplace and the source of water. Structures are typically two stories, have a symmetrical front facade with elaborate front doorways, often with decorative crown pediments, fanlights, and sidelights, symmetrical windows flanking the front entrance, often in pairs or threes, and columned porches.<br>Example: 112 Gibson Avenue, Page 28 | 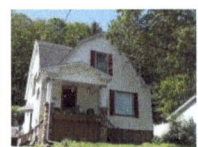 |
| **Queen Anne**, 1885-1900 – This style is distinguished by an irregular outline featuring a combination of an offset tower, broad gables, projecting two-storey bays, verandahs, multi-sloped roofs, and tall, decorative chimneys. A mixture of brick and wood is common. Windows often have one large single-paned bottom sash and small panes in the upper sash.<br>Example: 141 Lake Street, Page 44 | 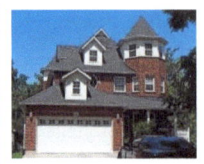 |

| | |
|---|---|
| **Regency Cottage**, 1830-1860 – This style originated in England in 1815 and spread to Ontario later in the 19th century as British officers retired to Canada. It is a modest one-storey house with a low-pitched hip roof and has a symmetrical front façade.<br>Example: 16 Mountain Street, Page 12 | 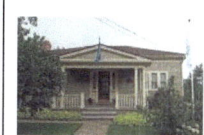 |
| **Tudor Revival** – exposed timbers with stucco infill, multi-paned windows.<br><br>Example: 20 Nelles Boulevard, Page 18 | 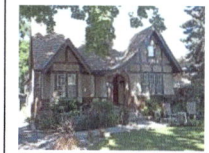 |
| **Vernacular/Traditional Mode** 1638 - 1950 Influenced but not defined by a particular style, vernacular buildings are made from easily available materials and exhibit local design characteristics.<br>Example: 13 Nelles Boulevard, Page 20 | 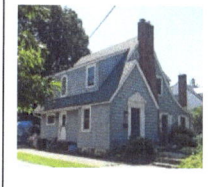 |

www.ingramcontent.com/pod-product-compliance
Lightning Source LLC
Chambersburg PA
CBHW041942240526
45473CB00033B/267